LIVING WITH

Co-occurring Addiction

AND

Mental Health Disorders

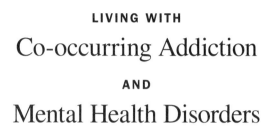

LIVING WITH

Co-occurring Addiction

AND

Mental Health Disorders

A Handbook for Recovery

Mark McGovern, Ph.D.

AND

Faculty from the Dartmouth Medical School

WITH

Scott Edelstein

HAZELDEN

Hazelden
Center City, Minnesota 55012
hazelden.org

Library of Congress Cataloging-in-Publication Data

McGovern, Mark.
    Living with co-occurring addiction and mental health disorders : a handbook for recovery / Mark McGovern with Scott Edelstein.
        p.   cm.
    Includes bibliographical references.
    ISBN 978-1-59285-719-7 (softcover)
    1. Substance abuse—United States. 2. Substance abuse—Treatment—United States.
    3. Dual diagnosis—United States. I. Edelstein, Scott. II. Title.
    HV4999.2.M37 2009
    362.29'16—dc22
                                                                                    2009032253

Editor's note
The names, details, and circumstances may have been changed to protect the privacy of those mentioned in this publication.

This publication is not intended as a substitute for the advice of health care professionals.

Alcoholics Anonymous, AA, and the Big Book are registered trademarks of Alcoholics Anonymous World Services, Inc. The Twelve Steps and Twelve Traditions are reprinted with permission of Alcoholics Anonymous World Services, Inc. ("AAWS"). Permission to reprint the Twelve Steps and Twelve Traditions does not mean that AAWS has reviewed or approved the contents of this publication, or that AA necessarily agrees with the views expressed herein. AA is a program of recovery from alcoholism *only*—use of the Twelve Steps and Twelve Traditions in connection with programs and activities which are patterned after AA, but which address other problems, or in any other non-AA context, does not imply otherwise.

13 12 11 10 09   1 2 3 4 5 6

Cover design by Madeline Berglund
Interior design by David Swanson
Typesetting by BookMobile Design and Publishing Services

*This book is dedicated to the men and women who suffer
from co-occurring addiction and mental health problems.
We hope our work can take each of them and their loved ones
a step closer to fulfilling the promises of recovery.*

Contents

List of Figures

List of Worksheets

Acknowledgments

The authors wish to acknowledge the invaluable writing, research, and scholarship offered by the following faculty from the Dartmouth Psychiatric Research Center, the Department of Psychiatry, and the Department of Community and Family Medicine, Dartmouth Medical School: Robert E. Drake, M.D., Ph.D., Vice Chair and Director of Research in the Department of Psychiatry and Director of the Dartmouth Psychiatric Research Center; Matthew R. Merrens, Ph.D., Co-director of the Dartmouth Evidence-Based Practices Center and Visiting Professor of Psychiatry; Kim T. Mueser, Ph.D., clinical psychologist and a Professor of Psychiatry and of Community and Family Medicine; and Mary F. Brunette, M.D., Associate Professor of Psychiatry at Dartmouth Medical School and Medical Director of the Bureau of Behavioral Health in the New Hampshire Department of Health and Human Services.

We are grateful to our community addiction and mental health treatment program collaborators, as well as the state agencies that provide funding for their treatment services. Without the guidance, input, and frontline experience of these many individuals, our understanding of the assessment and treatment process would be ill-informed at best.

Likewise, we are thankful for the editorial efforts and support of our colleagues and friends at Hazelden Publishing, most notably Richard Solly and Kate Kjorlien.

Lastly, we are indebted to the many men and women in recovery from co-occurring disorders. The lived experience and collective wisdom they freely offer grace every page of this book. Indeed and in spirit, they pass it on.

Introduction

How This Book Can Help

Let's listen in as several people talk about their lives:

> Rashid: It seems like I'm always arguing with people. I'm not a mean person, but many things people say just piss me off. Just yesterday a total stranger walked up to me and dissed my girlfriend, for no damn reason. What could I do but get in his face? Most of the time it's just words, but once in a while, especially after a few beers at Barney's, my neighborhood bar, it boils over into a fight.

> Natasha: My emotions rule me. I don't want them to, but they do. Sometimes I feel like I'm queen of the universe, filled with love and great ideas, and I want to hug everyone I meet and tell them about the incredible plans I have. Then, sometimes the very next morning, I can hardly get out of bed. Just making coffee seems like way too much work. Some days if it weren't for the meth, I'd stay in bed and not move all day.

> Seth: I'm the first to admit that I'm wound pretty tight. The endless details of life nag at me. Just leaving the house in the morning can set off a string of worries. Did I lock the back door? Did I turn off the stove after boiling my tea water? Did I remember to leave the bedroom door open for the cat? Sometimes I start out for work and then, a few blocks from home, I have to turn around and go back to

make sure everything's okay. I take lots of deep breaths—ten at a time—to help me relax. They do help a little. But what really helps calm me, especially at the end of the day, is a couple of bowls of weed. The only problem is that, lately, I've been having trouble sleeping without it.

Kim: The big problem with coke dealers is that they don't trust anybody. After you've been around one for a while, neither do you. It's not like I hang out with Brad, but when I go to his apartment every Monday to make a buy, often there's a game on his giant plasma TV, and he usually invites me to watch it with him. The problem is that lately I've got the feeling that someone's watching me. At first I thought it was the woman I see each morning walking her dog by the river. Now I wonder if it's my dry cleaner. Last summer she bought a house just around the corner, and now I run into her at least once a day—at Starbucks, at the drugstore, in the park across the street. It's possible that she's a narc staking me out, planning on arresting me. I know that sounds crazy, but just three weeks ago there was a big drug bust only four blocks away. I can't help but wonder if I'm next.

Alison: I don't know how my roommate does it. She always seems to know just what to say to people, how much to smile, what tone to use—all that stuff. I'm the opposite. If I meet somebody, once we've exchanged names and talked about what we do for a living, my brain locks up. I have no idea what to say. I get more and more anxious and embarrassed. Finally I make an excuse and get out of there. Sometimes I force myself to go to a party or art opening, but after ten or fifteen minutes, I just can't handle it. I get a drink, park myself in a corner, slurp the drink down, and repeat the process five or six times. Eventually I'm not anxious or embarrassed anymore, but I'm too wasted to do anything but call a cab, go home, and crawl into bed.

Each of these five people has what's called *co-occurring disorders* (or, sometimes, a dual disorders, a dual diagnosis, a co-morbid condition, or—as some recovering people refer to it—double trouble). Since *co-occurring disorders* is the most common variation, it's the term used most often in this book.

"Co-occurring" just means that someone has two or more disorders at the same time, like diabetes and high blood pressure. Each of the people quoted above has both a mental health disorder and a substance use problem (either substance abuse or substance dependence).

A reasonable amount of stress and a healthy physiology keep us sane and content. When things get out of balance, however, we can become absolutely miserable, and sometimes dangerous to ourselves or others. Medical professionals call this lack of balance a *mental health disorder.* Like many other disorders, it may require treatment. Also like many other disorders, it can be effectively treated in the vast majority of cases.

Although many people don't realize it, *substance dependence*—or, as it's more commonly known, *addiction*—is a type of mental health disorder. When someone can no longer control how much of a drug they use, or how much alcohol they drink, and they continue to use it even though it causes problems for themselves or others, they've got an addiction. This means they crave the addictive substance. Even though it causes them harm, this craving, in turn, leads to their uncontrolled drinking or drug use.

Co-occurring disorders occur when addiction gets mixed together with a second mental health disorder. This can be a powerful recipe for trouble—mostly to the person who has the disorders.

A second common type of co-occurring disorder affects people who *aren't* addicted, but who regularly abuse alcohol and/or other drugs. These individuals can also have depression, obsessive-compulsive disorder, or some other mental health disorder. Unfortunately, even when no addiction is involved, substance abuse typically plays havoc with people's lives and their ability to function. This can be doubly true for someone who already has a mental health disorder.

But there's a bright spot: many effective treatments are available for a wide range of mental health problems, for substance dependence or abuse, *and* for these disorders when they occur together.

Researchers now know that *most* people who have a mental health disorder have a substance use disorder—either substance abuse or addiction—as well. The inverse is true, too: 50 to 65 percent of people who receive services in addiction treatment centers also have a mental health disorder. And in any given year, eleven million North Americans suffer from co-occurring mental health and substance use disorders.

Let's not pull punches here: having co-occurring disorders is at least twice as difficult as having only one. But no one has only one big problem in life. Ask around; try to find someone with only one big life issue that regularly causes them problems.

Yet there is also some very good news for everyone with co-occurring disorders: there is lots of hope—and lots of help. More than two decades of intensive research has enabled professionals to create integrated treatment programs that address both sides of co-occurring disorders, at the same time, in the same place, and with the same group of professionals. These integrated programs have proven very effective, helping countless people to recover their health, their happiness, and their lives. This is true for every type of co-occurring mental health and substance use disorder.

This isn't cheerleading or wishful thinking. Scientists know success is possible because it has been evident in a wide range of clinical studies. Since this is a practical self-help book rather than a book for professionals, my colleagues and I won't trot out all the research—but everything in this book is based on studies of real people in real situations. It's all been tested and proven to be the world's "evidence-based practices": the things that work the best, and the most often, for the largest number of people.

The result of these evidence-based practices is that large numbers of people are now able to deal with every major type of co-occurring disorder. A great many are in successful recovery from their substance abuse and addictions. Many are in recovery from their mental health disorders. Others are able to control or manage their mental health disorders through proper treatment. And people from all of these groups have built or rebuilt meaningful lives.

This book contains the essence of what a small group of Dartmouth Medical School faculty have learned during more than twenty years of research involving people with co-occurring disorders and the professionals who treat them.

The single most important thing we've learned is that people who have a co-occurring diagnosis are more likely to get better, to get better faster, and to stay better, when both disorders are treated together, using a unified, integrated approach.

But "unified" doesn't mean a lockstep program. Over the years, we've also learned that one-size-fits-all approaches haven't yielded the best results. In fact, part of what does work best is letting each person make certain key decisions about his or her own treatment and recovery.

This book informs, empowers, explains what works and what doesn't, and offers a variety of positive choices and options. Its goal is to help people with co-occurring disorders to feel better, recover from their substance abuse or addiction, manage or recover from their mental health problems, build lives worth living, and be empowered advocates for their own health and sanity.

Accepting the Help That You Need

No one volunteers for a substance use disorder. No one signs up to have a mental health disorder. These are not life goals, not lifelong personal aspirations. Although we may choose to take our first drink, or our first hit on a joint, or our first line of cocaine, over time the element of choice or willpower seems long gone.

Admitting we have lost control of our substance use and meet diagnostic criteria for a bona fide disorder is difficult. It is difficult for a number of reasons. First, it seems like such a simple act: If we really put our mind to it, we could change. We could stop if we really wanted to. Unfortunately, even after repeated attempts, people who are addicted can't stop successfully (or can't stay "stopped"). Second, we may have shame and guilt about this loss of control. We think we must be weak, lazy, unmotivated, sleazy, a floozy, or a loser. But it simply means we have the disease of addiction, which is an equal opportunity destroyer. And third, substances like drugs and alcohol affect the brain. This is why we like them so much, but also why, over time, they have a deleterious effect on our memory, our judgment, our will, and our reasoning. Making the connection between the multiple life problems (failed marriages, lost jobs, relationship conflict, DWIs) and substance use should be obvious. But due to the brain changes associated with chronic substance use—the repeated ingestion of toxic substances—we don't see the cause-and-effect relationship. This needs to be pointed out to us.

Likewise, if we have the symptoms of depression or anxiety, avoid various situations and people, have nightmares and flashbacks of traumatic experiences, or rapidly cycle between intense euphoria and profound sadness, we want to believe these are simply extreme versions of normal human emotional experience. In some respects they are. However, these symptoms don't go away, or if they do, they come back with a vengeance. In addition, these symptoms interfere with our capacity to function normally. We have a hard time showing up for work, raising our hand in class, ordering in a restaurant, dating someone we find attractive, staying out of the hospital, or keeping a dollar in our bank account. We don't choose this kind of problem any more than an alcoholic or addict chooses theirs.

Remember, if you have a substance use problem, you are more likely to have a mental health problem and vice versa. So what if you have both? This is at least doubly hard to accept.

Once you do accept that you have a problem, you are only halfway there. You may be motivated for relief, to get better, to feel normal, but you'll need to take concrete steps.

No one gets better from a substance use disorder or mental health problem alone. Although there are some rare cases of individuals who overcome cancer or other serious medical problems without treatment, most of us would agree that trying to treat cancer alone would be preposterous. These percentages of "spontaneous remission" are also small for persons with co-occurring disorders, perhaps less than 5 percent. Don't we all want to be part of that 5 percent?

Professional help is available for people with mental health, substance use, and co-occurring mental health and substance use disorders. Sadly, the majority of people with these problems never seek this help. The barriers range from not believing they have a treatable condition, to cost concerns, to transportation problems, to not knowing effective help exists, to continuing to believe things will get better on their own. But they don't.

Treatment for substance use and mental health conditions is comparable in effectiveness to chronic medical diseases such as hypertension, diabetes, and asthma. People get help during acute or severe situations, get stabilized, and then get less intensive help in an ongoing low-maintenance way over time. They get checkups and have routine visits, monitor their functioning, take medication, and try to lead a healthy lifestyle. It's a big commitment, but one does what one must do. Most of us would consider these steps reasonable and normal if confronted with diabetes, hypertension, or asthma.

When it comes to mental health and substance use disorders, however, there is still a tendency to believe things like the following:

- "It's not that bad."
- "I am afraid of what it says about me and my image to others."
- "It won't work. My case is the worst ever."
- "It will be a hassle."
- "What will my family and friends think?"
- "What if the 'cure' is worse than the 'disease'?"

These common apprehensions are obstacles for everyone who eventually gets help. Some of us work through these hurdles faster than others. For some it takes days, for others, years.

If you are reading this book, you are at least open-minded enough to be considering your options. That's great. If you are concerned about a loved one and are reading this book on his or her behalf, that's equally great. Knowing the facts will empower you and enable you to help your loved one get help. We know that being in a relationship with a person with untreated co-occurring disorders is at least as unbearable as having the disorders themselves.

Thus, there are two steps to acceptance. The first is admitting you have a problem. The second is admitting you need help.

Getting the Most from This Book

This book contains information, guidance, and practical tools. Everyone can benefit from these tools, but readers who have already sought help, been assessed, and know about their diagnosis will already have much of the information in chapters 1 and 2. If so, feel free to go straight to chapter 3. (But you may still want to read or skim chapters 1 and 2, since these chapters probably contain some information that's new and useful.)

The same principle applies to anyone familiar with the basic information in any section or chapter: you can skip that material without worry or guilt. However, even when certain basic information may be familiar, the worksheets and other tools will likely be fresh and helpful. For many readers, the worksheets in this book may feel too small or uncomfortable to write on. Full-page worksheets are available for downloading at www.cooccurring.org.

No book can be everything to every reader, and each person's own recovery and ideal treatment plan will always be unique. What works—or even what might be ideal—for one person may not work at all for another. For this reason, you are encouraged to bring your own personal experience and judgment to each topic. You are also encouraged to discuss your concerns with a mental health professional, medical professional, or drug and alcohol counselor.

Lastly, although everything in this book is meant to be accurate and authoritative, this book does not—and cannot—offer medical or psychological advice, and it is not meant to be used in place of the guidance of a qualified substance use, mental health, or medical professional. *No one can effectively deal with any of these disorders alone.*

CHAPTER 1

Understanding the Situation

What Is a Disorder?

In the human body, a *disorder* is any ongoing condition that's less than healthy. If Sheila's arm often gets itchy and scaly, she's got a localized skin disorder. If Maurice is nearsighted, he's got an eye disorder. If Irina needs a couple of drinks before she can get out of bed and go to work each morning, she's got a substance use disorder. And if Yolanda often feels too anxiety-stricken to go to school, she may have a mental health disorder.

Let's look more closely at these last two types of disorders.

Substance Use Disorders

Just as there are big differences between an ordinary sore throat, a serious strep infection, and throat cancer, there are big differences between substance use, substance abuse, and substance dependence.

Substance use just means drinking alcohol or using another mood-altering drug. Although the drug may be illegal, one use alone doesn't constitute dependence. *Use* is different from *abuse*. For example, many people use alcohol, but don't abuse it. Someone *abuses* alcohol or another drug when their use of it persistently interferes with their ability to function, or with their social relationships, or with their own (or someone else's) health or safety. If Brad drinks three beers at a party, he isn't abusing alcohol. But if he drives home drunk, or if he picks a drunken fight with a stranger—or his partner—he's probably gone from use to abuse.

Alcohol or drug *dependence* (or *addiction*) is much more serious than abuse. It includes all the features of abuse—but, in addition, the person can't stop or control their substance use, even when he or she tries. The person will likely develop tolerance, using more and more to get high, and may experience withdrawal when he or she stops using or drinking.

If Perry often gets stoned and rowdy, he's got a substance abuse problem. If even when he tries, he can't stop himself from regularly getting stoned, rowdy, and in trouble, he's probably got a dependence problem.

Mental Health Disorders

Someone has a *mental health disorder* (sometimes called a *psychiatric disorder* or simply *mental illness*) if they have persistent or recurring problems with how they think, feel, or function.

If Katrina has trouble getting out of bed because she's taking antihistamines for her hay fever, or because her cousin died two days ago and she's grieving, she probably doesn't have a mental health disorder. But if Katrina can't get out of bed most mornings because it feels like way too much effort and she misses work because of it, she probably *does* have a mental health disorder.

The interaction of stress, environment, and physiological vulnerability is the central cause of mental health disorders. Decades of medical research have demonstrated that mental health disorders are comparable to other diseases, such as asthma, hypertension, and diabetes. They're not the result of moral failures, character flaws, a weak will, a lack of discipline, or parents who didn't read the right parenting manual. They're not punishment for sins, either. While genetics and brain chemistry factors influence all of us, mental health disorders are mainly the result of environmental factors and stress, just as diabetes may result if a vulnerable pancreas is exposed to unhealthy diet, lifestyle, or severe infection.

For a condition to be considered a disorder, it needs to last a certain length of time and not be a normal reaction to specific life events. If Mitch is having a tough month, it's normal for him to feel stressed out. But if his sense of impending doom never changes, even when things start going well for him, a mental health disorder could be at work.

What can cause a mental health disorder? All kinds of things: genetics; environmental factors, such as exposure to toxic chemicals or drugs or extreme and/or prolonged stress caused by trauma (often, but not necessarily, while growing up); physical disorders and conditions; serious injury, particularly to the brain; or, as is often the case, some combination of these factors.

How Are Disorders Treated?

Each disorder, and each combination of co-occurring disorders, is unique. So is each human body and psyche. This is why any disorder needs to be assessed by a professional (or a team of professionals), and why a unique treatment plan needs to be created for each person. Even if two people are prescribed the same medication, a 90-pound, 16-year-old girl may need a smaller dosage than a 240-pound, 40-year-old man. Similarly, two people might receive the same form of psychotherapy, but one may benefit from only nine sessions, while the other might need twenty or more.

Substance use disorders—particularly addiction—are often treated with one or more of the following:

- an addiction treatment and recovery program. Some of these are *inpatient* programs, which require people to live temporarily at a treatment facility; others are *outpatient* programs that allow people to commute.
- individual psychological, psychiatric, and/or drug and alcohol counseling.
- group therapy or counseling, usually with other people who have a substance use disorder.
- support groups. Many of these are freestanding Twelve Step groups such as Alcoholics Anonymous and Narcotics Anonymous; others are sponsored by hospitals, clinics, recovery centers, churches, or other organizations.
- medications. A variety of medications can reduce cravings and help people who abstain from drugs or alcohol to avoid a relapse. Some of these are tailored for alcohol dependency, others for drug dependency.

Mental health disorders are typically treated using one or more of the following (similar to the above treatment for chemical dependency):

- medications. These normally need to be prescribed by a psychiatrist or other medical doctor. (In some states, they can be prescribed under certain circumstances by other qualified professionals, such as nurse practitioners, physician assistants, or psychologists.) Contrary to what many people believe, most of the current medications for mental health disorders are entirely nonaddictive.

- individual psychological and/or psychiatric therapy.
- group therapy or counseling, often with other people who have the same disorder, for example, post-traumatic stress disorder.
- support groups sponsored by hospitals, clinics, churches, associations (Anxiety Disorders Association of America, National Alliance on Mental Illness, etc.), and other service organizations.

Until relatively recently, people with co-occurring mental health and substance use disorders were rarely treated for both disorders together, in an integrated fashion. Much more often, professionals would first try to help clients recover from one disorder, then move on to the other. Or they'd only treat one disorder on the incorrect assumption that it was the "root" or "core" or "primary" disorder. In many cases, professionals wouldn't even know about the existence of one or more of the co-occurring disorders. It shouldn't be surprising that the rate of successful treatment for these co-occurring disorders wasn't very high.

When only one part of co-occurring disorders is treated, the problems caused by the untreated disorder often get in the way of working successfully on the other disorder. For example, if someone with both alcoholism and depression is treated just for his or her depression, the person may continue drinking alcohol, which is a depressant and which interferes with the effectiveness of antidepressant medications. On the other hand, if the person is treated just for alcoholism, he or she may readily relapse and use alcohol to medicate the depression. Or the person may simply be too depressed to get off the couch and go to Alcoholics Anonymous meetings.

It is now known that if professionals just treat the psychiatric part of co-occurring disorders, the whole person will usually get worse; if they just treat the substance use, the whole person will also usually get worse. People do best when both disorders are treated together—ideally by the same group of professionals, in the same setting, following a single integrated recovery plan.

Effective treatment for disorders of all types also includes education and skill building. Whatever disorder someone may have, they can benefit greatly from learning how to best manage it, cope with it, and control or deal with its symptoms.

Understanding Mental Health Disorders

When people first learn—or suspect—that they have a mental health disorder, they can have a wide range of reactions.

Some feel a great sense of relief. *Oh, so that's what's been going on! Man, it was hard not knowing why I felt so strange or acted the way I did. But now that I know what the problem is, I can get it treated and start feeling better.*

Others feel scared, just as they would in facing any other disorder. *Is it serious? Will I get better? Will I get worse? What are my chances of being cured?*

Both of these are normal and appropriate reactions—and it's not unusual to feel both ways at once.

There's a third group of people, though, who at first feel ashamed or blame themselves for their disorders. *It's my own damn fault. If I were stronger and more disciplined, like my sister, I wouldn't have let this happen.* But this self-blame is entirely unjustified. Decades of medical research have shown without a doubt that *anyone* can contract a mental health disorder, just as anyone can get cancer or fall down and break their wrist.

Many people are also afraid of what others—friends, family, neighbors, co-workers, and employers—will think about their disorders. They worry that others will look down on them as weak or crazy or screwed up.

These fears are partly—but only partly—justified. On the one hand, it is now known unequivocally that having a mental health disorder doesn't make someone less of a human being. It doesn't mean that they're bad, evil, wimpy, sinful, or shameful. It means something's not working as it should and they need treatment. On the other hand, it's also true that some people don't yet understand this—and their own ignorance can cause them to ridicule, pity, or stigmatize others. But they're just plain wrong. They don't have their facts straight.

You can't stop these people from judging you and telling you what to do, but you don't have to take them seriously. Here are the sorts of things you might hear from them, and some possible ways to respond.

- *"So, are you like those who get locked up, put in straitjackets and stuff?"* "Not really. I've got a disorder, like asthma or fibromyalgia or arthritis, and I'm getting treated for it. With the right treatment, my brain chemistry will stabilize, and I can live a normal life, like anyone else."
- *"It's really a spiritual problem. You don't need doctors or medications. Just give it all over to God."* "I'd need a doctor if I broke my leg, wouldn't I? Well, right now some part of me is broken. Professionals can help me fix it, just like a doctor would set a broken bone. But I'm not denying the power of prayer. In fact, I'd be grateful if you'd pray for my healing and quick recovery."
- *"You've always been too sensitive, scared of a lot of things. Forget the doctors and*

appointments. Just straighten up and grow a backbone!" "I'm not scared of the truth, and the truth is I've got real stress and things happening in my body that need correcting. Professionals can help me with that, just like my dentist can help by filling cavities. Cavities don't just straighten up and grow fillings. It's the same for this—it won't correct itself without some help."

The point here is that no one with any kind of disorder—whether it's kidney stones, diabetes, panic disorder, or bipolar disorder—should avoid getting the professional help they need because of what others say, think, or believe.

Common Mental Health Disorders

Medical and mental health professionals divide mental health disorders into five basic types:

1. Anxiety disorders, including panic disorder, social anxiety disorder, generalized anxiety disorder, post-traumatic stress disorder, and obsessive-compulsive disorder

2. Mood disorders, including depression, bipolar disorder, seasonal affective disorder, dysthymia, and cyclothymia

3. Personality disorders, such as borderline personality disorder, narcissistic personality disorder, histrionic personality disorder, and paranoid personality disorder

4. Organic disorders or disorders caused by physical illnesses, such as Huntington's disease, Parkinson's disease, systemic lupus erythematosus, and a variety of neurological disorders

5. Thought disorders, such as schizophrenia, schizoaffective disorder, and delusional disorder

The *Diagnostic and Statistical Manual of Mental Disorders,* a well-known reference book for mental health and addiction professionals, includes and classifies substance use disorders with the above disorders.

The great majority of people with co-occurring disorders have one (or more) of the anxiety or mood disorders and a substance use disorder. Smaller numbers of people with co-occurring disorders have manic disorder (also called *mania*) or schizophrenia or schizoaffective disorder and a substance use disorder. These are the types of co-occurring disorders discussed in this book.

Interestingly, many people who have one mental health disorder also have one or two others—which means that they literally have not only double trouble but also triple trouble, or even quadruple trouble. Modern therapies and medications, however, can often treat multiple conditions effectively.

Let's take a quick look at the most common co-occurring mental health disorders—as well as a few that are somewhat less common.

Bipolar Disorder

Sometimes known as *manic depression,* this disorder causes extreme mood swings between mania and depression, usually with symptom-free periods in between. In the manic phase, people with bipolar disorder typically experience euphoria, grandiosity, excitement, overconfidence, and a decreased need for sleep. They may speak or move rapidly and may easily become irritable, angry, aggressive, and/or easily distracted. In the depressed phase, they usually feel hopeless, sad, discouraged, fatigued, and/or empty; they have trouble sleeping or else oversleep; they quickly lose or gain a great deal of weight; they have trouble focusing or concentrating; they become easily frustrated; they lose interest in things and activities they used to care about; and they may have persistent thoughts of death or suicide. Each phase typically lasts for weeks or months. Hallucinations or delusions may accompany either or both stages. In any given year, about 2 percent of all people experience bipolar disorder (estimates range from fewer than 1 percent to 2.5 percent).

Cyclothymia

This is sometimes described as a milder version of bipolar disorder. As with bipolar disorder, it involves cycling through two phases. In the first, people experience euphoric highs and boosts of energy, and require less sleep than usual; in the second, they experience an ongoing mood of negativity and sadness. Neither phase is as severe as in bipolar disorder. However, untreated cyclothymia tends to be chronic and long lasting; in fact, to be diagnosed with the disorder, a person must have experienced it for at least two years, with periods of relief lasting no more than two months. In any given year, less than 1 percent of all people experience cyclothymia (estimates range from 0.4 percent to 1 percent).

Depression

Unlike ordinary sadness (feeling depressed temporarily about some situation or event), major depression (sometimes called *clinical depression*) involves intense and prolonged feelings of worthlessness, hopelessness, emptiness, helplessness, regret, and/or guilt. Often these are accompanied by thoughts of death or suicide. Depression can also create a variety of physical symptoms, including pronounced changes in sleep, energy, and/or appetite; difficulty thinking, concentrating, or remembering; a lack of interest in previously pleasurable activities; and persistent headaches, digestive disorders, and/or pains that do not respond to treatment. In any given year, about 7 percent of all people experience major depression. People with depression are not just "bummed out" or "feeling the blues." Depression as an illness is serious and requires treatment.

Dysthymia

Sometimes referred to as low-grade depression, dysthymia is a persistent, chronic form of mild to moderate depression. Because it is less severe than clinical depression, people who have dysthymia often experience it not as a disorder, but as their normal state of being. Symptoms include long-term feelings of hopelessness, sadness, and/or pessimism; trouble sleeping and/or oversleeping; extreme fatigue; difficulty concentrating or focusing; irritability; indecisiveness; constant self-criticism; and feelings of guilt or worthlessness. In any given year, about 2 to 3 percent of all people experience dysthymia.

Generalized Anxiety Disorder (GAD)

People with GAD worry excessively and chronically over everyday concerns such as health, money, family, and work. Often their thoughts get stuck on the potential for disaster in normal situations. People with GAD cannot shake these worries even though they know they are largely unwarranted. Physical symptoms of GAD include restlessness, edginess, fatigue, difficulty concentrating, irritability, muscle tension, and trouble falling or staying asleep. In any given year, about 1 percent of all people experience GAD.

Obsessive-Compulsive Disorder (OCD)

People with OCD often say that their minds are stuck in a loop: a single thought, urge, or image repeats over and over, and they cannot let go of it. Often this is combined with obsessive feelings that things must be done in a certain exact way. These compulsive thoughts typically lead to compulsive actions, such as excessive hand washing; repeatedly checking, ordering, cleaning, or arranging things; doing the same task or activity over and over, often in a ritualistic way; and repeating the same phrase again and again. In any given year, about 2 percent of all people experience OCD.

Mania (or Manic Disorder)

Although this disorder can appear on its own, it is more likely to occur as part of bipolar disorder (see page 15). Symptoms include grandiosity, high energy, restlessness and/or a reduced need for sleep, rapid speech, racing thoughts, impulsivity, creative and/or disjointed thinking, excitability, and irritability. *Hypomania* is a mild form of this disorder.

Panic Disorder

People with this disorder experience sudden panic attacks: episodes of extreme fear and terror lasting from a few minutes to an hour. They may also feel as if they are dying, going crazy, or having a heart attack. People with panic disorder can be so shaken by these episodes that they withdraw and shut themselves off from the outside world. In any given year, 1 to 2 percent of all people experience panic disorder.

Social Anxiety Disorder

People with this disorder experience intense anxiety in ordinary social situations and interactions. Making a phone call, attending a meeting or a party, making a purchase at a store, or asking a stranger for directions can feel intensely stressful and difficult. People with this disorder also worry that others are constantly watching them and judging them negatively. In the presence of others, they may experience physical symptoms such as a pounding heart, sweating, shaking, blushing, muscle tension, an upset stomach, or diarrhea. Not surprisingly, people with social anxiety disorder tend to stay home and avoid social situations; they also tend to feel lonely, because they avoid contact with others. In any given year, about 6 percent of all people experience social anxiety disorder—a surprisingly high percentage.

Post-traumatic Stress Disorder (PTSD)

PTSD is the result of one or more traumatic events. These events can range from being sexually abused as a child, to being in an automobile accident or natural disaster, to being in a combat or war zone. People with this disorder often feel vulnerable and out of control, or as if their lives are in danger. They also typically reexperience the traumatic event over and over in memories, dreams, and flashbacks. Not surprisingly, they may try to avoid people, places, and situations that remind them of this traumatic event. People with PTSD often feel constantly vigilant or on guard and may be easily startled or upset. Other common symptoms of PTSD include constant fear or tension, restlessness, insomnia, irritability, and/or poor concentration. In any given year, about 2 percent of all people experience PTSD.

Schizophrenia

This serious disorder profoundly affects people's behavior, thinking, emotions, and functioning. It includes misperceptions, distorted reality, delusions, hallucinations, mood changes, bizarre behavior, and a general loss of contact with reality. Schizophrenia can be managed and successfully treated, but it is not usually cured.

Schizoaffective disorder is itself a co-occurring disorder. It comes in two forms: a combination of schizophrenia and major depression, and a combination of schizophrenia and bipolar disorder.

In any given year, about 0.2 to 0.4 percent of all people (between one-fifth of 1 percent and four-tenths of 1 percent) experience schizophrenia. About half that percentage— one-tenth to one-fifth of 1 percent—experience schizoaffective disorder.

Understanding Co-occurring Disorders

It's not always easy to tell if you have co-occurring disorders. Of course, in some cases it may be obvious to you (*Jeez, when did I start worrying myself sick? And when was the last time I made it through a whole day without doing coke?*) or to the people around you (*"Sandra, you're starting to smell like a walking bong. And your plans don't sound ambitious; they sound completely off the wall. When did you last feel good about yourself?"*).

More likely, though, you'll have a vague sense that something is wrong, but won't know what. Or you'll feel anxious, or afraid, or sad, or depressed, or guilty, or angry, and not know why. An important relationship may suddenly fall apart, seemingly without warning. Or maybe you're already aware of one of your problems, but one day you realize that something else must be going on as well.

People with co-occurring disorders typically develop them in one of three ways:

1. They first develop a mental health problem and then turn to drinking or drugs in an attempt to reduce their symptoms and feel better. For example, many people with an anxiety disorder will drink alcohol to help themselves relax and calm down. Over time, this attempt at self-medication can turn into an addiction.

2. They first develop an addiction, which in turn induces a mental health problem. For example, the regular use of certain mind-altering drugs can sometimes be a partial cause of major depression, anxiety, or panic disorder. In other cases, the mental health disorder is latent or relatively minor, and the addiction becomes the catalyst that brings it out or makes it worse.

3. Some people are genetically more vulnerable to addiction, or to a mental health disorder, or to both—just as some people are more likely than others to lose their hearing as they age.

Other people may be more vulnerable to co-occurring disorders because of their environment or life experience. For example, Kim's parents were both cocaine addicts; she naturally became curious about the drug at an early age and soon developed her own addiction to it. Chauncey served in the military and was captured and briefly tortured; he developed symptoms of PTSD when he returned home. In college, Adrienne fell in with a group of friends who regularly indulged in binge drinking; eventually her friends grew out of the alcohol abuse, but Adrienne found she couldn't stop. All of these people are more vulnerable than most to co-occurring disorders.

Although drug or alcohol use can sometimes temporarily reduce the symptoms of certain mental health problems, substance use actually has exactly the opposite effect. For example, if Suzette has depression, even two drinks might make her depression much worse or make her feel suicidal. Frederico has generalized anxiety disorder, and for him even a few puffs on a joint ratchet up his anxiety to an almost intolerable level.

Then there's the issue of prescription medications. A glass of wine will take the edge off Jacob's post-traumatic stress disorder, but now that Jacob has begun taking a medication to help his PTSD, he can't drink alcohol. That same glass of wine, mixed with the medication, could make his PTSD worse, or at least render the medicine ineffective. (This is yet another reason why it's essential to treat both parts of co-occurring disorders together, in an integrated way.)

Most doctors now know that a person with a mental health disorder is more likely than other people to also have a substance use disorder. And if the person has a substance use problem, he or she is more likely than the average person to also have a mental health disorder. Statistically, someone with schizophrenia or bipolar disorder has a one in two chance of acquiring a substance use disorder; someone with depression or an anxiety disorder has a one in three chance.

There's a positive side to this, though. If Mariana has both alcoholism and depression, there's a three in five chance that when she stops drinking, the depression will go away.

How Do You Know If You Have a Mental Health
or Substance Use Disorder?

Sometimes professionals can determine a great deal from an initial assessment. That's why, if you suspect you might have co-occurring disorders—or even just a substance use problem or just a mental health disorder—your best first step is to get a thorough assessment.

There are online tests or screenings you can take with complete anonymity. Some of them are quite good and have proven validity and reliability. That means you can count on them to assess accurately what they are intended to assess. You might also visit the National Institute on Drug Abuse (NIDA) at www.nida.nih.gov or the National Institute on Alcohol Abuse and Alcoholism (NIAAA) at www.niaaa.nih.gov. You'll find excellent information to help you better understand alcohol and drug abuse and dependence. If you're wondering about your mental health, visit the National Alliance on Mental Illness (NAMI) at www.nami.org. To learn more about both mental health and substance use disorders or co-occurring disorders, visit the Substance Abuse and Mental Health Services Administration (SAMHSA) at www.samhsa.gov. All of these Web sites are good starting points for any individual to begin looking at his or her own mental health and substance use.

If you suspect you have one or both disorders, it's recommended that you contact a qualified professional immediately for an assessment, which is explored in the next chapter.

CHAPTER 2

Getting an Assessment

What Is an Assessment?

An assessment is a professional evaluation of someone's mental health, general physical health, and alcohol and/or drug use. An assessment can determine whether someone has a mental health disorder, multiple mental health disorders, a drug use problem, an alcohol use problem, or some combination. It's also the necessary foundation for developing an effective recovery plan.

An assessment may take place in a clinic, treatment center, hospital, or mental health professional's office. The client and the professional meet for about one to two hours, during which the professional asks the client questions about his or her life. These typically include several dozen standardized questions, as well as a less structured interview about the client's health, lifestyle, thoughts, emotions, concerns, and willingness to recover. All answers are kept strictly confidential, except in cases where clients seem likely to harm themselves or others.

In some cases, this meeting with a professional may be preceded by a brief preliminary screening, either in person or by phone, conducted by a nurse or staff person. In other cases, the client may be asked to answer some initial questions in writing before the face-to-face interview begins.

Here are some typical assessment questions:

- In the past two weeks, have you been less able to enjoy the things you used to enjoy?
- In the last six months, have you worried excessively?
- In the past month, did you do something repeatedly without being able to resist doing it? What?
- Have you ever heard things other people couldn't hear, such as voices?
- Have you ever had a drink or used drugs first thing in the morning, to steady your nerves or get rid of a hangover?
- Have any of your family members ever had a drinking or drug problem?
- During the past week, how often did you feel lonely?

The professional does more than just listen to clients' answers. Professionals also pay attention to clients' speech, body language, demeanor, and facial expressions. Do they have trouble sitting still? Do they have difficulty concentrating? Do their hands tremble? Is their speech slurred?

Most high-quality assessments for co-occurring disorders also include a urine test (for opiates, cocaine, cannabis, barbiturates, amphetamines and methamphetamine, and other common mind-altering drugs) and/or a breath test (which measures blood-alcohol concentration). Sometimes there is a physical exam and/or blood is drawn. In rare cases, even a hair sample may be taken and analyzed.

In any assessment, honesty and forthrightness are crucial. If a client lies or withholds essential information, the assessment is not likely to be altogether accurate, and any proposed treatment may be inappropriate and unhelpful.

After the assessment interview, the client should find out when the results will be available and make an appointment to discuss those results with the professional face-to-face. Usually the results will be ready in a few days, and sometimes they'll be available immediately.

Who Should Conduct an Assessment?

Only someone who is trained in *both* the mental health and substance use disorder (also called *addiction, chemical dependency,* or *substance abuse*) fields can conduct a thorough and accurate assessment of any co-occurring disorders. For this reason, it's best to seek an assessment from a professional or program that specializes in integrated treatment for co-occurring disorders. Sometimes programs may note they have dual diagnosis "capable" or dual diagnosis "enhanced" services.

There are three different ways to locate one of these professionals or programs:

1. Someone who has a regular physician can ask for a referral. However, it's essential to explain, "I think I may have co-occurring disorders, so I need someone who's an expert in assessing both substance use and mental health disorders."

2. Someone who has health care coverage can contact their insurer or HMO and request a referral. Once again, it's essential to explain, "I think I may have co-occurring disorders. I may have a drinking problem *and* a mental health problem, so I need someone who has expertise to assess both substance use and mental health disorders." In some cases, the insurer or HMO will make a direct referral; in others, the client may be required to visit a physician, psychiatrist, psychologist, or social worker, who will authorize the referral.

3. The Web offers an ever-growing number of sites for programs and professionals that can provide an assessment; these can be located by googling *dual diagnosis, dual disorders,* and *co-occurring disorders.* However, information obtained from the Web may not always be reliable, so it's recommended that you check the authenticity of any information and resources you find on the Web with your family doctor.

Insurance Issues

Although many health plans cover assessments, some do not. Some first require that a deductible be fulfilled; others exempt assessments from those deductibles. Some require co-payments; some don't. And, of course, plans change their coverage from time to time.

Clients should check with their insurers or HMOs before making an assessment appointment. This means calling the customer service department and saying, "I'm concerned that I may have co-occurring disorders—what's sometimes called a dual diagnosis. That's a mental health disorder plus a chemical use problem. I want to get myself assessed for this possibility, and then get treatment as appropriate. What coverage does my plan have for this assessment? Do I need a referral from a doctor or psychologist? Do I need a preapproval from you?"

It *always* makes sense for people with health care coverage to have their assessments billed to their insurers, *even if the assessment isn't covered.* While the insurer won't pay any of the bill, it may nevertheless have negotiated a reduced fee with the professional or program, thus reducing the out-of-pocket cost to the client.

For an *uninsured* person, the cost of an assessment can vary widely, depending on who performs it and what organization, if any, they work for. In addition, many professionals and organizations charge according to a sliding scale, based on the client's income. It is strongly recommended that clients find out the actual out-of-pocket cost in advance—and comparison-shop if it sounds too high. There are also many clinics and programs for people who have no insurance and who qualify, which are funded by the U.S. government and by individual states.

Assessment Results

At the end of the session or at a follow-up meeting, the professional presents the client with the assessment results, answers the client's questions, and recommends what to do next. This meeting normally takes about sixty to ninety minutes.

The results of an assessment typically include

- whether alcohol and/or other mind-altering substances were found in the client's lab results.
- diagnosis of the client's substance use disorder, if any—including its form, its severity, and its potential dangers.
- diagnosis of the client's mental health disorder, if any—including its form, its severity, and its potential dangers. If the client has more than one mental health disorder, each one is diagnosed.
- overall analysis of the client's current condition and situation.
- analysis of the client's motivation to change mental health or substance use issues and to use professional help to do so.
- options for treatment. This often includes a referral to a particular type of professional, program, or agency. Some clients may be offered a list of recommended therapists, programs, or agencies from which they can choose. Other clients may be told, "Our clinic/agency/hospital offers this form of treatment, and it does an excellent job. Would you like to learn more about it?" There's nothing wrong with exploring this option—but it's also perfectly acceptable to look into other programs as well. In fact, as discussed in chapter 4, comparison shopping is encouraged.

- options for one or more prescription medications. In some cases, if the client wishes, a qualified professional can write an appropriate prescription on the spot.
- other recommendations. These might include lifestyle changes, temporary hospitalization, or reading materials.

Sometimes, a tentative treatment plan is recommended at this meeting. However, normally a final plan is determined later, once the client has reviewed all the options and made a choice that fits his or her personal preferences and chances for success.

A small percentage of people who get assessed learn that they *don't* have co-occurring disorders after all, but just a mental health disorder or just a substance problem. This is generally good news, because it means they can choose from a larger number of programs, options, and therapists. Their next steps are the same, however: finding the right program and/or a good therapist, and stepping onto the path of recovery.

Emotional Responses to Assessment Results

Many people react strongly when they first get their assessment results. Here are some typical responses:

- Oh, man, what a relief. I thought I had just plain lost my marbles.
- Thank God the docs know what I've got and know what to do about each disorder. Now I have hope again.
- I had no idea this was such a common condition. I thought it was some weird thing unique to me. It really helps to know that there are millions of people just like me out there.
- I'm scared to death. I never imagined it was this serious.
- So now it's official: I'm screwed up. God, I'm embarrassed (ashamed, disgusted with myself, etc.).
- Oh, crap. *Now* what am I going to do?
- I'm devastated. What will my partner think?
- *Please* don't tell my family (my boss, my co-workers, etc.). If they find out, I'll be up a creek without a paddle.
- I'm an action-oriented person, and I want to put this behind me ASAP, so let's start treatment right away. What's the first step?

- I'm at your mercy. I'll do whatever you say. Tell me what to do next.
- Hell, no! You've got me completely wrong. I'm getting out of here.
- Everything you say makes sense—but I'm just not ready to deal with it right now. I've got so many other things on my plate already. Maybe I'll start treatment in a few months, after I finish my MBA.
- I'm not sure. Something about this doesn't feel right. I want to check with someone else and get a second opinion.

It's not unusual to have a strong emotional reaction in this situation. But people should not take those reactions too seriously; it's important to feel them fully, but not to cling to them. Clients need to be patient, curious, and open-minded at this stage. As they allow their treatment and recovery to unfold, they discover that many of their worries fade away, and that events play out far more favorably than they imagined. As for those whose initial response is relief and trust, these feelings tend to persist throughout treatment and recovery.

How Reliable Are Assessments?

Can an assessment be partly or completely wrong? Yes. It's unlikely, but it does happen. No assessment, no matter how carefully designed, will ever be perfect—and even well-trained professionals make mistakes.

Since a client has everything to gain from an accurate assessment, and a great deal to lose from an inaccurate one, *anyone* who feels that some of his or her assessment results aren't right should ask about them. Questions might include the following:

- You said that I'm _____ or that I have _____. I'm not sure what you really mean by that. What am I missing about this?
- Can you tell me how you came to this conclusion? What test results did you rely on, and what other evidence pointed in this direction?

Clients who genuinely feel that their assessment results aren't accurate have the right to get a second opinion from a different professional, program, or organization. Clients should be encouraged to do this, just as they should be encouraged to get a second medical opinion whenever *any* test result or diagnosis feels wrong.

In requesting a second opinion, however, people need to keep the following points in mind:

- A second assessment may require the advance approval of their health insurer or HMO. In some cases this second assessment may not be approved. (It can still be done, of course, but at the client's expense.)
- Problem minimization is a part of some mental health disorders, as well as a common symptom of substance use problems. Sometimes what feels all wrong at first may turn out to be correct after all. (Issues of denial often arise and get dealt with in treatment and recovery.)
- If the results of a second assessment mirror those of the first, it's almost certain that both assessments are accurate. But if they do differ significantly, it's essential to discuss both sets of results with a professional.
- If a client isn't forthcoming, truthful, and accurate in his or her assessment interview, the results are likely to be inaccurate. A client who didn't tell the whole truth should say so now, ask to be reassessed, and provide new, accurate, and complete information this time.

What It All Means

Whatever results an assessment yields, it's never the end of the world. In fact, every assessment has the potential to lead to hope, healing, and recovery. This is true no matter how many disorders a person has, and no matter how serious they are.

No one with co-occurring disorders is alone. Whatever combination of disorders people have, they share that combination with hundreds of thousands (and perhaps millions) of other people of all backgrounds from all parts of the world, including executives, doctors, farmers, nurses, politicians, community leaders, housewives, teachers, and members of almost every other profession.

Healing and recovery are *always* possible.

CHAPTER 3

Physiology, Stress, and Environmental Factors

The Biochemistry of the Brain

We enter the world at birth with a genetic makeup that determines a number of things about us. These include not only basic things like eye and skin color and even bone structure, but also risk factors for certain medical conditions, such as cancers or heart diseases. Our temperament—including how we react to stimuli or new situations, or even our baseline mood—also has genetic determinants. These mental or emotional characteristics have been challenging for scientists to study since they are also affected by environment, including the time we spend in our mother's womb, as well as early experiences in infancy and childhood. Ongoing research with genomes is striving to disentangle the specific profiles of DNA that might account for certain emotional and behavioral characteristics.

In the meantime, our best understanding of the origins of mental health issues, and of substance use problems, involves starting with genetic or biologically determined factors. These may include genes that affect the development of brain anatomy, function, and resiliency. This complex interplay of factors includes childhood and life history, as well as environmental factors, such as poverty, academic opportunity, family support and encouragement, peer group influences, religious beliefs, and culture.

To put it simply, substance use or mental health disorders develop via a combination or interaction of biologically determined factors, stress, and environmental dimensions. Any might be considered risk or protective factors. We may have genetic or environmental factors that place us at a greater or lower risk for mental health or substance use problems. Added to these factors is stress. The degree of pressure placed on us can trigger or exacerbate risk or protective factors. Even with a boatload of risk factors, humans can be amazingly resilient and rise above their biological and life circumstances to be healthy and successful.

Psychological and Biological Treatments for Co-occurring Disorders

Although researchers are presently less clear about the origins or causes of co-occurring disorders, they are more clear about the treatments.

Treatment for mental health or substance use disorders may involve medications. These medications help to address the biological factors influenced by genetics at birth and over time by environmental or stress factors. Treatments may also be psychological or focused on our social or living environments. These treatments, often called "psychosocial," are designed to help us manage stress, cope with our biological vulnerabilities, and learn more effective ways of coping with stress and interacting with other people in the world.

Research tends to show that both medication and psychosocial treatments are effective. In fact, for many disorders, the combination is the most effective.

It is often tempting to imagine that there is a pill or "silver bullet" that will make us feel calm, attractive, whole, safe, connected, confident, secure, potent, or energetic. Perhaps the quest for this magic pill contributes to what draws people into using substances such as alcohol or drugs.

That being said, medications have been developed to counterbalance biological vulnerabilities (either inherited or acquired) so that a person has a level playing field and a chance at life. These medications, coupled with psychosocial treatments, provide people with co-occurring disorders an excellent opportunity at full recovery.

Guidelines for Prescribing Medications for Co-occurring Disorders

It will be important to discuss with your treatment provider what makes medications a potential option for you. Here are some of the factors a professional considers when determining if and what medication to prescribe, what dosage to prescribe, and how often (and for how long) a client should take it:

- how effective the medication is likely to be for that client
- potential side effects and how the medication interacts with other prescription drugs and with common over-the-counter remedies, including alcohol
- how potentially addictive the medication is (this is a great concern for any client who already has a substance use problem)
- client's current mental and physical condition
- client's current alcohol and drug use, abuse, or dependency
- client's sex, age, weight, and height
- client's occupation, hobbies, and plans for travel (some medications can be dangerous for people who fly planes, climb mountains, race cars, etc.)
- client's allergies or disabilities
- other medications the client takes and any negative reactions to medications in the past
- what medications the client's insurer or HMO covers (and doesn't cover) and out-of-pocket cost for the medication

No one knows in advance which medications will work best, or what the ideal dosage is, for any one person. An experienced professional can make a good guess, but there's always a trial-and-error period that can last a few days, weeks, or even months.

For some people, this trial-and-error period can be smooth and easy. For others, it can create confusion, frustration, pain, or fear. A medication (or combination of medications) may not work as well as expected; it may take awhile to have much effect; strong and unpleasant side effects may appear; and, in some cases, a medication may make the client's condition worse.

Because of all these variables, people who take prescription medication should closely monitor their own bodies, thoughts, and emotions; understand that finding the right medication (or combination of medications) and the right dosage may take some time; and inform the prescribing professional immediately of any and all problems or side effects. And, if they experience a genuine emergency because of their medications, they should get help immediately or dial 9-1-1.

The issue of lag-time can be particularly challenging. Some medications begin having positive effects within a few hours or days, but others take much longer—up to several months—to be fully effective. When clients see few or no positive effects for weeks or months, they are often tempted to stop taking their medications because they "aren't working." Or, they may want to take larger doses, or take the medication more often, in the hope of seeing some quick benefit. *Any of these actions can do serious harm.* It's essential that, instead, they stay the course, be patient, and let the medications do their job over the long term. If they are concerned that the medication isn't working, they should discuss the matter with the professional who prescribed it.

Common Medications Used to Treat Co-occurring Disorders

Seven general types of prescription medications are commonly used to treat co-occurring disorders:

1. Antidepressants
2. Antipsychotics
3. Anti-anxiety and sedative medications
4. Hypnotics (medications that induce and maintain sleep)
5. Mood stabilizers and bipolar medications
6. Medications for alcohol addiction
7. Medications for drug addiction

Let's take a closer look at each group. Except where noted, none of these medications is addictive.

Antidepressants

Despite their name, these medications are usually effective in treating both depression *and* anxiety.

Antidepressants can help people with dysthymia, bipolar disorder, and major depression. They can reduce or eliminate symptoms such as sadness, low energy, difficulty sleeping, sleeping too much, appetite loss or gain, difficulty concentrating, negative thoughts about oneself and the world, and an inability to feel pleasure.

Antidepressants can also reduce or eliminate symptoms such as fear, nervousness, muscle tension, and obsessive thoughts. They can therefore help people with anxiety disorders, such as obsessive-compulsive disorder, post-traumatic stress disorder, panic disorder, generalized anxiety disorder, and social anxiety disorder.

Antidepressants affect the brain's *neurotransmitters*—biochemicals that are responsible for feelings, thoughts, and behavior. In particular, antidepressants alter the balance of the neurotransmitters *serotonin* and *norepinephrine*.

There are four types of antidepressants: *SSRIs (selective serotonin reuptake inhibitors), SNRIs (serotonin and norepinephrine reuptake inhibitors), MAOIs (monoamine oxidase inhibitors),* and *tricyclic antidepressants.* Each alters the balance of the brain's neurotransmitters in a unique way.

Antipsychotics

Antipsychotics are primarily used to reduce or eliminate hallucinations (seeing or hearing things others can't), delusions (fixed false beliefs), disorganized or confused speech, and bizarre or confusing behavior. Antipsychotics are also called *major tranquilizers* or *neuroleptics.*

Antipsychotics are commonly used for people with schizophrenia or schizoaffective disorder. However, antipsychotics are also used for some people with bipolar disorder or mania. Antipsychotic drugs can reduce or eliminate irritability, euphoria, rapid speech, a decreased need for sleep, grandiosity, impulsivity, extreme or foolish risk taking, and excessive spending.

There are two general types of antipsychotic drugs. *Conventional antipsychotics* act primarily on the neurotransmitter known as *dopamine*; *atypical antipsychotics* affect both dopamine and serotonin levels.

Anti-anxiety and Sedative Medications

Anti-anxiety medications help reduce agitation, fear, worry, anxiety, and muscle tension. *Sedatives* also ease many of these same symptoms, but their primary benefit is in helping people fall asleep and stay asleep. Some people with co-occurring disorders have trouble falling asleep, staying asleep, or both; sedatives are sometimes prescribed for these individuals. However, these drugs can be addictive, so they are prescribed less frequently than many other medications for people with co-occurring disorders.

Researchers don't yet fully understand how anti-anxiety and sedative medications work. However, it is known that—like antidepressants and antipsychotics—they alter the balance of certain neurotransmitters.

Hypnotics

Hypnotics are medications that induce and maintain sleep. These drugs can be very helpful for people with sleep problems, but some are not advised for people with a risk for substance abuse or dependence.

There are four basic types of hypnotics: *benzodiazepines; melatonin* and related drugs; *sedating antihistamines;* and *sedating antidepressants.* The first group, the benzodiazepines, can be easily abused and are sold on the street, so they are generally not prescribed for people who have a history of substance use disorders. However, the other three types of hypnotics are safe, nonaddictive, and widely prescribed.

Mood Stabilizers and Bipolar Medications

Mood stabilizers are used to treat mania and hypomania, bipolar disorder, major depression, dysthymia, severe anxiety disorders, schizophrenia, and schizoaffective disorder. They can reduce or eliminate symptoms such as irritability, euphoria, rapid speech, a decreased need for sleep, grandiosity, impulsivity, extreme or foolish risk taking, and excessive spending. For people with bipolar disorder, major depression, or dysthymia, they can reduce or eliminate the depressive symptoms: sadness, low energy, difficulty sleeping, sleeping too much, appetite loss or gain, difficulty concentrating, negative thoughts about oneself and the world, and an inability to feel pleasure.

Researchers are still unsure exactly how mood stabilizers and bipolar medications work in the brain. However, it is known that—like antidepressants, antipsychotics, and anti-anxiety medications—they change the balance of certain neurotransmitters.

There are two general types of mood stabilizers: *lithium* and *anticonvulsants.* Each is especially effective with certain mental health disorders—and, in some cases, with specific varieties of those disorders.

For people with mania and bipolar disorder, some of the antipsychotic drugs listed earlier can also serve as mood stabilizers.

Medications for Alcohol Addiction

People in recovery from alcohol addiction commonly experience strong cravings for alcohol. Three medications—*naltrexone, acamprosate,* and *disulfiram* (more commonly known by the brand name *Antabuse*)—can deter the impulse to drink, lessen cravings, prevent relapses, and, when relapses do occur, make them briefer and less severe.

Naltrexone reduces the activity of *endorphins* (naturally occurring opiates) in the brain and reduces the pleasurable feelings associated with drinking alcohol.

Acamprosate appears to lower the level of the neurotransmitter *glutamate* and raise the level of the neurotransmitter *GABA* (*gamma-aminobutyric acid*). An imbalance between these two neurotransmitters is believed to play a role in alcoholism. Like naltrexone, acamprosate reduces the pleasurable feelings that result from drinking alcohol.

Disulfiram (Antabuse) blocks the body's production of an enzyme called *aldehyde dehydrogenase.* Drinking even a tiny amount of alcohol then creates a cluster of painful symptoms, including shortness of breath, headache, nausea, and rapid heartbeat. People taking disulfiram must be careful to avoid vinegar, certain mouthwashes, aftershave, and rubbing alcohol, because even touching a small amount of one of these substances can induce the same unpleasant symptoms.

Medications for Drug Addiction

A variety of medications exists to help treat opiate addiction, and many promising new ones are in development. The two medications most commonly used are *methadone* and *buprenorphine.* Both are often prescribed for people in recovery from addiction to heroin, morphine, Vicodin, opium, codeine, and other opiates.

Both methadone and buprenorphine are addictive; someone who takes either drug regularly and then suddenly stops will experience withdrawal symptoms similar to what they would experience with an opiate. However, people who take a fixed dose of either drug (methadone does eventually cause tolerance) do not need gradually larger doses over time to get the same benefit. This is why using either of these medications as prescribed is considered a step toward recovery from addiction. It's also far less dangerous (and expensive) than an opiate dependency.

Methadone appears to lower the level of the neurotransmitter glutamate in the brain. This reduces the cravings for opiates, minimizes the high that opiates can provide, and helps to prevent relapses.

Buprenorphine appears to simultaneously mimic the activity of endorphins in the brain and decrease the activity of actual endorphins. This eliminates cravings for opiates by essentially satisfying the brain's desire for them.

Dosages of either drug are closely and carefully monitored by a professional, because too much of either one can lead to illness or death.

Some Important Reminders about Medications

Although medications can be of great value to people with co-occurring disorders, as mentioned earlier, they are rarely silver bullets. Just taking a pill won't clear up every part of the disorder. In the overwhelming majority of cases, a carefully designed treatment program, which includes talk therapy and other forms of support, is necessary.

This being said, it is essential to consider medications as a viable option for effectively treating either or both the mental health or substance use disorders. Do not be ashamed of taking medications as prescribed. Your recovery is no better or no worse than anyone else's for doing so. But it's also important to keep in mind that most medications treat only one part of co-occurring disorders. For example, antidepressants can help people with depression or dysthymia, but they won't do a thing about their substance use disorder. Similarly, disulfiram (Antabuse) and methadone are quite effective in reducing people's cravings for addictive, mind-altering drugs, but they have no direct effect on other mental health disorders. This is why most people with co-occurring disorders are often prescribed a combination of medications.

All medications have the best chance of working when clients take the proper prescribed dosage at the prescribed times and intervals. Doing otherwise may not only keep the medication from working but also could create (or worsen) serious physical illness or mental health problem.

Here are some ways to ensure you're taking the right dosages of the right medications at the right times and intervals:

- Include the medications as part of a normal daily routine—for example, just after showering, while making morning coffee, or immediately after supper.
- Post a medication schedule on the bathroom mirror, on the outside of the refrigerator door, on the car dashboard, and/or in other prominent places.
- Set an alarm clock or timer to go off at appropriate times.
- Ask family members or friends to provide verbal reminders at appropriate times, either in person or by phone.

While full recovery from co-occurring disorders includes no longer abusing drugs or alcohol, it's not uncommon for people to resume (or continue) drinking or drugging sometime during treatment. Nevertheless, even then, it's *extremely* important that they continue to take their medications. They may feel guilty that they've "been bad" or "blown it" by not staying clean and sober. But they haven't blown it. By continuing to take the right medications in the right amounts and at the right times, they continue to support the proper balance of brain biochemicals. This will help them feel better and will make it much easier to end their relapse and return to sobriety. (There are two important exceptions here. Drinking alcohol while taking disulfiram/Antabuse or using heroin, morphine, Vicodin, or any other opiate while taking methadone or buprenorphine can lead to serious illness or even death.)

As always, people taking any prescription drug should avoid taking *any* additional medication not specifically prescribed for them—even a nonprescription, over-the-counter drug—without first checking with their doctor. The wrong combination of medications can render one of them useless—or, in some cases, cause pain, illness, or mental instability.

Once a medication starts to work, clients often feel so much better that they're tempted to take fewer medications or to take them less often. *This is most often a huge mistake.* There's a paradox here. Clients feel like they don't need the medication precisely *because* they are taking the medication, which is working the way it should. If they decide to stop taking the drug, they also stop supporting their own mental health and will start to feel worse again.

Lastly, what about alternative "medications"—dietary supplements, homeopathic remedies, herbs, essential oils, and the like? The best of these, used properly, may boost the body's ability to stay healthy, and they are often—but not always—compatible with prescription drugs. Again, check with your doctor. These alternatives shouldn't be used in place of medications prescribed by a medical doctor or other professional, because they have not been tested using the same government standards and research protocols as medications.

Medications are one essential part of most people's recovery plans. In the next two chapters, we'll look at the other two crucial elements: an appropriate treatment program and a caring, capable therapist who feels right for you.

Chapter 4

Finding the Ideal Treatment

Getting Started

Because there are so many combinations of dual or co-occurring disorders, and because the symptoms and severity can vary widely from person to person, there is no simple chart that says, "People with co-occurring disorders A and B need treatment C." It's never that easy. Treatment *always* needs to be geared to each individual. Professionals consider not only each client's disorders and symptoms but also a variety of other factors. These factors might include their previous treatment response, age, sex, cultural background, and/or religious beliefs; their health care plan; where they live; what language they're most fluent in; and so on.

Nevertheless, some generalities about treating co-occurring disorders do apply:

- The most successful treatments address all parts of the disorder together, in a single, integrated way—usually in the same setting, with a single professional or group of professionals.
- The most successful treatments usually combine medication with *talk therapy:* focused, regular discussion and interactive learning under the guidance of one or more professionals. Talk therapy is particularly valuable in helping people make long-term positive changes in their lifestyle, thinking, and decision making.

- A client's own commitment to recovery and willingness to change, learn, and grow also make a huge difference. People who take treatment seriously and come to it with open minds do far better than those who resist it, distrust it, or make only a halfhearted commitment to it.

- Caring, intelligent, well-trained professionals are the beating heart of successful treatment. Any treatment program or recovery plan is only as good as the professionals who implement it. The caring and respectful relationship between the provider and the client is critical to a successful recovery.

- The support of loved ones makes a huge difference. When someone's family and/or friends actively supports their recovery, they are likely to recover faster and more fully. In contrast, when people don't lend their support—or even get in the way of the person's recovery—successful treatment usually requires much more effort from the client.

At first glance, the number of treatment options may seem overwhelming. In practice, though, choices are often easy to make, for three reasons:

1. When a client meets with a professional to discuss assessment results, the professional typically recommends options for treatment and some therapists and/or programs that can best provide it. The professional may even say, "I work with people who have co-occurring disorders, and I can take on a new client. Would you like to work with me?" or "The clinic I work for offers an integrated treatment program specifically for co-occurring disorders. Would you like to speak to someone here about it?"

2. In many locales, treatment options are limited. There may be only one fully integrated treatment program nearby, or there may be only one or two mental health professionals who offer an integrated approach. (Getting treatment in a location away from home is always an option, of course.)

3. The client's health insurance plan or HMO may cover a limited range of treatment programs and/or professionals.

However wide or narrow the options, the client almost always has choices to make—ideally in close consultation with a mental health or addiction professional and the client's family.

A Treatment Program, One-to-One Therapy, Group Therapy,
or a Combination

All of these are built around talk therapy. Although there are distinct benefits to each option, they aren't either/or choices. For example, integrated treatment programs normally include a good deal of group therapy and some one-to-one therapy as well.

Some people with co-occurring disorders can do best when they get started with a formal treatment program, such as an inpatient residential program, plus medication when appropriate. Once they have completed the formal program, which typically lasts thirty to ninety days with an array of educational and therapeutic components, they and their professionals can together decide on next steps. To learn exactly what therapies are involved in any formal treatment program, it is best to contact the center itself.

For people with serious co-occurring disorders, it is often best to start with *both* a formal treatment program and ongoing one-to-one therapy, as well as medication. Using therapy, support groups, and medication simultaneously helps clients stay focused and on track—as well as clean and sober—during the all-important initial weeks of recovery.

Some people with mild co-occurring disorders need nothing more than regular one-to-one talk therapy—or some combination of one-to-one and group therapy. However, this option is recommended only when an assessment clearly suggests that the option is sufficient. While one-to-one and group therapy may be more convenient and flexible than a formal treatment program, they're considerably less effective for some people.

A Fully Integrated Treatment Program, a Mental-Health-Centered Program, an
Addiction-Centered Program, or Addiction-Only or Mental-Health-Only Programs

Chris wants to buy a house. First she looks at a newly built home with central air-conditioning. The roof and walls are well insulated; the unit is neatly tucked away in an unobtrusive spot; the air intake is near the garage; and the house has a single thermostat that controls both the heat and the A/C.

Next Chris looks at an older home in which central air-conditioning was installed five years ago. Parts of the unit take up much of the middle of the basement, making the space less usable. The air intake is located near the front door. The house has radiators, which take up space, *and* ducts in the walls. There are two separate thermostats: one for heating, another for cooling. The house isn't very well insulated.

Then Chris looks at a third house, which doesn't have central air-conditioning at all, but comes with four window air conditioners. They're noisy and expensive, and they obstruct the view from several windows.

What does this have to do with treatment programs for co-occurring disorders?

A *fully integrated* or *dual diagnosis enhanced* treatment program is like the first house. It's *designed* for people with co-occurring disorders. It looks at mental health disorders and substance use issues in an integrated fashion. These integrated programs are strongly recommended over all other treatment program options.

In our research, we found that in 2009, less than 10 percent of all programs were integrated across representative states in the United States. However, the field is slowly becoming increasingly sophisticated, so more and more programs are quickly developing co-occurring capability. These programs describe themselves as *enhanced* programs providing *integrated treatment* or *integrated services.*

Many other treatment programs for co-occurring disorders resemble the second house Chris looked at. They're either mental health treatment programs onto which addiction treatment programs have been grafted, or addiction treatment programs with mental health components added on.

There's a way to tell these from fully integrated programs: their program descriptions on the Web and in printed materials won't use the words *integrated treatment, dual diagnosis enhanced services, integrated services,* or *fully integrated.* However, keep in mind, there are currently no mandated or regulatory standards that regulate the names/terms programs can use to describe themselves.

The third house Chris looked at is a bit like participating in two simultaneous treatment programs, one for mental-health-only disorders, and the other for substance-use-only disorders. Each can be helpful, but they're not designed to work together. Their combined cost can also be high.

An Inpatient or an Outpatient Program

Inpatient or *residential* means "in residence": people live and eat together in a treatment facility, 24/7, for the length of the program. Accommodations are typically reminiscent of college dorms, though in some facilities each person has his or her own room. Participants typically spend six to eight hours per day, five days a week, in treatment-related activities. Residential treatment programs can run for as few as 30 or for as many as 90 days or even more. Inpatient hospital programs typically are less than one week, and probably no more than two. Treatment and recovery, of course, continue well after completion of the inpatient or residential program. (Some inpatient programs are located in a hospital, either on a medical/surgical unit or on a psychiatric ward. Most programs are not hospital-based, but they do provide residential care.)

Outpatient, intensive outpatient, or *day treatment* means "commuter" or "nonresidential." Participants commute to and from the treatment site, just as they would with work or school, and usually spend anywhere from one hour per week to nine or twelve hours a week in intensive treatment. Intensive outpatient programs typically meet for about three hours a day, several days a week. Most outpatient programs run 90 to 120 days, some run six months, and a few run for a full year. Treatment and recovery normally continue long beyond completion of the formal program. These programs are called "intensive outpatient programs" or IOP. *Outpatient* does *not* mean "less serious" or "less focused." Quite the contrary. The same commitment, effort, participation, and willingness to change are required for both types of programs (outpatient or residential). People in outpatient programs don't get to skip sessions because they have errands to run or their child is performing in a school play. Participants must devote themselves honestly and earnestly to their treatment and recovery, just as they would in an inpatient program. Just showing up—or trying to slide by with minimal effort—won't cut it.

The term *partial hospital* or *day treatment* can be a bit confusing. Nonresidential treatment programs may be offered either during the working day or in the evening; sometimes both day *and* evening programs are called day treatment programs, to differentiate them from inpatient programs.

Allowing clients in outpatient programs to live in their own homes provides convenience, but this arrangement can be as much a drawback as a benefit. In an inpatient or residential program, everything is carefully controlled: the setting, the people, the food, and, especially, the lack of temptations. Alcohol and mind-altering drugs aren't available at any price, and no one in the vicinity is using them. Family members, friends, or neighbors who might be negative influences aren't around, either. Paradoxically, outpatient programs often require more effort and discipline than inpatient programs, because people in outpatient programs go home every night to the same home, neighborhood, situations, and stresses that may have contributed to their co-occurring disorders.

The one other difference between inpatient and outpatient programs is cost: outpatient programs are generally less expensive and thus affordable for many more people.

Finding the Right Treatment Program

Most clients' assessment results include a discussion about treatment options and choices, including potential programs or a referral to one program in particular.

Googling *dual diagnosis, dual disorders,* or *co-occurring disorders,* along with the word *treatment,* will bring up dozens of programs. (Each term tends to bring up a somewhat different list.) Adding *integrated* to the search criteria will narrow that list; so will adding a state or metropolitan area, or *outpatient, intensive outpatient, residential,* or *inpatient.*

It can also be helpful to specify particular disorders, such as alcoholism and social anxiety disorder, PTSD and cocaine abuse, or addiction and trauma. Although most treatment programs for co-occurring disorders cover a wide range of mental health disorders and substance use problems, a small number focus on specific combinations. A fully integrated program that focuses entirely on the relevant disorders may be ideal.

It's worth looking carefully at each program's Web site, but since terms such as *co-occurring* or *dual diagnosis* are not standardized or regulated, it's even more important to call and ask questions. Here are some suggestions:

- Does the program offer fully integrated addiction *and* mental health treatment and services? (If the representative doesn't know, or doesn't immediately understand the question, the answer is almost certainly no.)
- Has the program ever been assessed by an objective outside evaluator and been categorized as *dual diagnosis enhanced* or *dual diagnosis capable*?
- I have these disorders: _____. Does your program work with people who have this combination of disorders? Do you have a program that focuses specifically on this combination?
- Is the program inpatient or outpatient—or do you offer both options? What hours does the program run each day? How many days per week?
- How many days/weeks does the program take?
- Where is the treatment facility located? Is it accessible by public transportation? Do you offer programs at multiple locations?
- Can you briefly outline the components of the program for me and send me more information in a booklet, on a CD, or both? Where can I find more information about the program on the Web?
- Is it possible to visit the treatment center and get a quick tour?
- Are alumni from the program willing and able to talk about their experience in the program?

- Will I have my own room, or will I share it with someone else? (for inpatient programs only)
- What is the cost? If I can't afford your program, will you recommend others?
- Do you take (name of health care plan)? Does the plan pay for everything, or will I be responsible for a portion of the charges? How much? (Note: Even if the program does not accept a particular health care plan, that plan may still pay all or part of the cost; however, the client must pay for the program, then file a reimbursement claim. Ask if a case manager can help handle these issues for you.)
- Is there a sliding fee based on income? Do you have a reduced price for people without health care coverage? Is a payment plan available?
- I have the following health, mobility, or dietary concerns: _____. Can you accommodate me?
- I have the following handicap or disability: _____. Can you accommodate me?

Insurance Considerations

Before beginning any form of treatment, prospective clients need to check with *both* their health care plans *and* any professionals and/or treatment programs they are considering. Because coverage and procedures vary widely from one health care plan to another, it's important to learn exactly what is and isn't covered, what limits apply, and what preapprovals are needed. Many treatment centers now have full-time staff or case managers devoted to handling insurance matters. Here are some questions to ask a health care plan's customer service representative:

- Is an inpatient or residential treatment program covered? Does coverage end after a certain number of days? How many? Is this limit per year or for the whole course of treatment? Is there a daily maximum that the plan will pay?
- Is an outpatient treatment program covered? Does coverage end after a certain number of days or sessions? How many? Is this limit per year or for the whole course of treatment? Is there a daily maximum that the plan will pay?
- Is individual counseling covered? How many sessions will the plan pay for? Is this per year or for the whole course of treatment? Is there a per-session maximum that the plan will pay?
- Are there any limitations on which programs, professionals, and organizations

I can use? (Some plans only pay for services from programs, organizations, and professionals in their own provider networks. Others allow clients to use out-of-network providers, but may charge a co-pay. Still others require clients to pay for out-of-network providers' services from their own pockets, and then submit claims for full or partial reimbursement.)

When a particular service isn't covered, clients should request the provider bill the health care plan directly whenever possible, because the plan may have negotiated a lower rate for its members.

Some therapists in private practice do not accept any insurance or HMO plan. However, many plans will nevertheless reimburse clients for part or all of those therapists' charges if they pay those charges, then submit a reimbursement claim.

Federal legislation passed in 1996 and 2008 requires insurers and HMOs to cover mental health and substance use disorders in the same way they cover physical health conditions. Although this is very good news, it does not automatically guarantee coverage for any particular form of treatment. The only way to be sure is to check with the insurer or HMO. Further changes in funding of treatment as well as payment for medical interventions may make some of these concerns moot. Again, be sure to check with your doctor and HMO.

Occasionally, health care plans inappropriately deny coverage to their members—sometimes in error, sometimes deliberately. These denials can and should be challenged in writing—usually in a letter, though some plans have official complaint or challenge forms. Many plans have an ombudsman whose job is to handle these challenges. Whether the challenge comes in a letter or on a complaint form, it's important to explain the situation fully, provide all the relevant information, and point to the applicable language in the policy or statement of coverage.

Another option is to have a lawyer write such a letter. A lawyer's signature and letterhead are one way of conveying very serious intent—as well as the consideration of legal recourse.

Although insurers and HMOs are often portrayed as heartless and money grubbing, many health care plans will change their decisions when presented with reasonable arguments, especially for tried-and-true services that are not terribly costly.

It's sometimes true that squeaky wheels get more grease. Clients who make a reasonable case may get turned down once or twice, but get approved for coverage when they challenge the decision a third or fourth time.

Clients who feel they have been unfairly denied coverage can also file a complaint or appeal with their state's attorney general's office, health department, office of managed health care, or other appropriate office. This may lead to mediation, binding arbitration, or some other form of resolution outside the courts. Another option—normally reserved only for serious misconduct—is filing a lawsuit against the health plan.

Tips for People without Health Care Coverage

Many low-income people without health insurance are eligible to receive government-sponsored health care at no charge. Many different programs exist; all are administered by the individual states, and options and coverage differ from state to state. Details on eligibility and enrollment are available through each state's department of mental health and/or addiction services, or related departments of public health.

In many states, people who can afford commercial health care coverage, applied for it, and were turned down because of preexisting health conditions can purchase coverage from a state-sponsored plan. Again, programs and coverage differ from state to state. Details are available from each state's department of health.

In most states, HMOs are required to have an annual open enrollment period, usually lasting about a month, during which anyone can enroll, regardless of their health status or preexisting conditions. Plans and coverage differ from state to state and HMO to HMO. More information is available directly from HMOs.

Interestingly and perhaps surprisingly, in our research we found that there are many integrated state-funded programs for people without health insurance. These public-funded programs are often as available to people *without* insurance as private-sector programs are available to those with insurance.

The All-Important Human Element

Treatment of co-occurring disorders is fundamentally about human interaction, human understanding, and person-to-person help and support. A good deal of help and support can come from a trusted psychologist, social worker, psychiatrist, family doctor, or other mental health/addiction professional.

Part of finding the ideal treatment, then, includes finding the right professionals, making the most of their talents, and building a strong and trusting client-therapist relationship. In chapter 5, we'll look at how to do each of these.

CHAPTER 5

Choosing and Working with a Therapist

The Value of One-to-One Therapy

For the great majority of people with co-occurring disorders, one-to-one talk therapy (or *psychotherapy*) is an important part of recovery. Some begin this one-to-one work at the beginning of treatment; others take it up only after completing a formal treatment program; and still others may prefer to remain with one therapist apart from any formal treatment program.

Most of us are familiar with the stereotypical image of a therapist sitting in a chair, taking notes, while the client lies on a couch and talks about his or her childhood. Although a small group of therapists (called *psychoanalysts*) may work this way, the great majority don't follow this model (called *psychoanalysis*).

In the twenty-first century, most therapy has a much more practical orientation. Its goal is to help people heal and recover from disorders, and/or live fuller, happier, more integrated lives. While a cure isn't possible, the goal of therapy is to help clients best manage their disorders.

Therapy seems to be a one-sided relationship: it's the therapist's job to focus on the client and the client's needs, not the other way around. Nevertheless, therapy is a team effort toward the common goal of improving the client's life. For therapy to work, both the client and the therapist must contribute time, effort, and careful attention. And the client needs to feel safe with the therapist and trust the therapist's motives and expertise—though this trust may take some time to develop.

One-to-one therapy for people with mental health and/or substance use disorders doesn't just take place in therapy sessions. Most therapists will ask their clients to work on certain things between sessions. This helps people to make changes and recover more quickly. In fact, research shows that people who do this work between sessions do better over time. In fact, many therapists give clients assignments between sessions.

Therapy is confidential. Every conversation between a therapist and client is private. The only time therapists will break this confidence is if they believe their clients may be at immediate risk to harm themselves or someone else.

This confidentiality includes not revealing who their clients are. If Marlene is Babette's therapy client and they run into each other at the gym, Babette will act as if she doesn't know Marlene unless Marlene greets her or initiates a conversation.

Recovery from co-occurring disorders isn't easy. Successful one-to-one therapy involves learning new information, skills, ways to think and choose, and ways to act. Both the client and the therapist need to be forthright, honest, and engaged. It's not enough for either person just to show up, or for therapy sessions to focus on whatever is on the client's mind.

Talk therapy can sometimes be painful, too, just as physical therapy can be painful for someone recovering from a physical injury. Also like physical therapy, talk therapy has big long-term payoffs: better mental health, greater happiness and serenity, and fewer difficulties over the long term.

What Is a Therapist?

The term *professional* is used often in this book. It's a catchall term that refers to mental health professionals, chemical dependency counselors, medical doctors, physician assistants, osteopaths, nurses, and physical therapists—basically, anyone who treats people with mental or physical disorders. The widely used term *clinician* means the same thing.

The term *therapist* is more specific: it refers to any mental health professional who provides talk therapy. Anyone with one or more of the following titles and degrees is qualified to provide one-to-one talk therapy.

- Drug and alcohol counselor. This person is trained to provide one-to-one counseling and guidance in the field of substance abuse (also called *addiction*). They may have an associate (two-year) degree, bachelor's (four-year) degree, or master's degree in addiction studies and chemical dependency counseling, as well as a license or certification; or they may have an associate or bachelor's or master's degree in psychology plus additional training and certification in the addiction field. Generally, these counselors are not skilled in treating co-occurring mental health disorders unless they also have additional training or a master's degree or special certification in psychology, social work, family therapy, or psychiatric nursing. States have individual licensing requirements for these professionals.

- Clinical psychologist (or licensed psychologist). Most clinical or counseling psychologists have doctoral degrees in psychology, though in some states a master's degree in psychology is sufficient.
- Social worker (or clinical social worker or licensed social worker or licensed clinical social worker). This person has a master's or doctoral degree in social work, with an emphasis in mental health counseling.
- Family therapist (or couples and family therapist; marriage and family therapist; marriage, family, and child counselor; etc.). This person has a master's or doctoral degree in family therapy, or a master's or doctoral degree in psychology or social work, plus graduate-level training in family systems.
- Clinical specialist (or clinical nurse specialist). This person has a graduate degree in a mental health field from a school of nursing.
- Psychiatrist. This is a medical doctor who has completed a residency in psychiatry. Although some psychiatrists do one-to-one therapy, most focus primarily on prescribing, evaluating, and adjusting medications.

These professionals may or may not have advanced training or certification in substance use disorders and/or co-occurring disorders.

The abbreviations for these professionals' degrees, licenses, and titles form a thick alphabet soup: A.A., A.S., B.A., B.S., C.D.C., C.F.T., C.N.S., C.S., C.S.W., D.S.W., F.T., L.P., L.A.D.C., L.P.C., Lic.S.W., L.C.S.W., L.M.F.T., M.A., M.D., M.F.C.C., M.F.C.T., M.F.T., M.S., M.S.N., M.S.W., Ph.D., Psy.D., and R.N.

Some therapists are generalists; others have a particular focus or speciality, just as some medical doctors specialize in pediatrics or gynecology or psychiatry. Therapists can specialize in

- certain types of client
- specific mental health disorders

- specific forms of substance use disorder
- particular mental health concerns

Some therapists view therapy—and their clients—through a particular lens. Others are more eclectic, drawing from a variety of approaches based on the needs of each client. And some therapists don't even think in terms of approaches. "I do whatever the client needs and the situation demands," many of these therapists say. "I don't use prepackaged solutions."

A therapist with a particular approach will still adapt it to each client and situation. And therapists who say they avoid prepackaged solutions won't hesitate to use a standard therapeutic technique when the situation calls for it.

Each therapist also has a personal style. Some are friendly and informal, others quite formal. Some are blunt and assertive, others tactful and restrained, and still others empathetic and warm. Some mostly ask questions and listen; others do a fair amount of talking. Some share examples from their own lives; others never say a word about themselves.

Even therapists who share the same basic approach may vary greatly in their styles and in how they interact with their clients. This is as it should be, because therapists are human beings, not therapy delivery units.

What Matters and What Doesn't?

Although every therapist should have the proper training and degree(s), the letters after someone's name rarely reveal much about their skills or talent. A person with a D.S.W. or Ph.D. or Psy.D. isn't necessarily a better (or worse) therapist than one with an M.A. or M.S.W.

Four things do matter a great deal, however: (1) a therapist's specialty and experience, (2) their therapeutic approach, (3) their personal style and fit with the client, and (4) their talent and skill as a professional.

Specialization

A cardiologist knows far more about the heart than a family practice physician. In the same way, a therapist who specializes in co-occurring disorders—or who has a great deal of professional experience with these disorders—may be far more helpful than a generalist or a counselor with experience only in, say, addiction or mental health disorders.

It's not that generalists aren't capable or helpful. But a specialist is likely to have deeper, more detailed, and more up-to-date knowledge on the subject.

One client, Sawat, learned from her assessment that she has panic disorder and is alcohol dependent. Now she wants to find a therapist. Sawat might rank potential therapists this way:

#1. Those who specialize in treating co-occurring panic disorders (or anxiety disorders in general) and alcoholism
#2. Those who specialize in treating co-occurring panic disorders (or anxiety disorders in general) and substance use disorders
#3. Those who specialize in treating mental health disorders and alcoholism
#4. Those who specialize in treating panic disorder
#5. Those who specialize in treating anxiety disorders
#6. Generalists
#7. Therapists with other specialties

Sawat lives in Manhattan, so she is able to find several therapists who fit the first category. But Edwin, who has the same co-occurring disorders, lives in a small town in Arizona. He has fewer options nearby: a therapist who specializes in treating co-occurring disorders, one who specializes in treating anxiety disorders, and three talented generalists. Sometimes people just end up choosing someone a friend or family member may have had a good experience with, whether for a similar problem or not.

Approach

For people with co-occurring disorders, a variety of therapeutic approaches have proven particularly effective. Motivational enhancement therapy (MET), motivational interviewing (MI), cognitive-behavioral therapy (CBT), or a blending of these therapies and others have been effectively integrated into many therapists' approaches. As a client, feel free to ask what practice or approach your therapist uses with his or her clients. Some of these therapies will be discussed later in this book; for now here are two often-used therapies:

1. *Motivational enhancement therapy (MET)* or *motivational interviewing (MI).* This therapy focuses on helping clients examine the reasons for changing

either their mental health issues or substance use. Sometimes we want to get rid of a problem without doubt; other times giving up a so-called problem may be scary. MET is an approach the therapist uses to make the pros and cons of change clear in clients' minds, so that clients can feel more certain and committed to the choices (and tasks) it takes to change when they're ready.

2. *Cognitive-behavioral therapy (CBT).* How we think often drives how we feel. Many people with co-occurring disorders experience a cascade of negative thoughts, which in turn creates negative feelings and actions. CBT helps clients examine how they tend to think in certain predictable but inaccurate ways (which therapists call *cognitive distortions*). The therapist then helps the client learn new ways of processing experiences in order to create more accurate and more positive ways of thinking and acting.

Style and Fit

A therapist's style matters. Yet style isn't a matter of right or wrong, but of what works for the individual client. A style that works beautifully for Gwyneth might rub Murray the wrong way.

In evaluating a therapist's style, each client is their own best expert. If a therapist's style feels wrong, unhelpful, or uninspiring, then a successful therapeutic relationship is very unlikely, and it's wise for the client to find someone else.

There's also the question of fit, which therapists call the *therapeutic alliance.* Fit is a combination of rapport, engagement, comfort, and trust.

When a client and a therapist are a good fit for each other, the client is relaxed and forthcoming in the therapist's presence. The client finds it easy to hear and understand what the therapist says. There is a meeting of minds, a shared energy, and a coming together as a team to support the client's recovery. When the fit is wrong, the client is guarded or awkward or confused, or feels that the therapist doesn't truly listen or understand.

By the second or third therapy session, it's usually clear whether or not there's a good fit between a client and a therapist. When the fit isn't right, it usually makes sense for the client to end the relationship and find a new therapist.

However, some words of caution are necessary here. Many people get along well with their therapists until they reach an emotionally difficult or painful spot. Then, instead of temporarily accepting that pain or difficulty and working through it, they announce that the fit is wrong, end the relationship, and go hunting for someone else—all in an attempt to deny or avoid their own pain. Eventually they will need to face that pain if they are to move forward in their recovery.

Ability

Although therapy is a team effort, clients of highly skilled therapists generally do better than those who are unskilled.

When a therapist isn't very talented, his or her clients soon realize it. They think, *He's a great person, and I enjoy being with him, but he's missed some pretty obvious connections.* Or, *I always come out of sessions feeling good, but I'm not sure she's helping. She never really challenges me, and I haven't changed my life or my thinking in any important way.*

It makes sense to leave an untalented therapist and find another, just as it makes sense to leave a hairstylist who gives raggedy-looking haircuts.

Personal and Cultural Background

It's not uncommon for clients to look for—or insist on—a therapist who shares their race, gender, religion, or sexual orientation. Making such distinctions in hiring an employee is illegal and unfair, but it's entirely fair and appropriate when choosing a therapist. In fact, these commonalities can encourage the building of trust and rapport.

Here are some other legitimate requests:

- "I want a therapist who's a working mother, like me, so I know she understands my situation from the inside."
- "I want a therapist who speaks Spanish."
- "I want a therapist who's a Somali immigrant like me, so they'll really understand the challenges I face."
- "I want a therapist who has recovered from their own co-occurring disorders."
- "I don't have a car, so I need a therapist whose office I can bus or walk to."

Of course, asking for something is different from being able to get it. If there are only two therapists in town who are Somali immigrants, and neither one is taking on new clients, then it's time to move to plan B. This might involve looking for a therapist who has worked with immigrants from a variety of countries.

It boils down to this: your beliefs about factors that can jump-start or strengthen a therapeutic relationship are legitimate.

Shopping for a Therapist

Finding the right therapist sometimes requires some trial and error—and/or some comparison shopping.

Many people have found good therapists by asking for recommendations and referrals from

- other people they know with co-occurring disorders
- the professionals who did their assessments
- their physicians or other health, mental health, or addiction treatment professionals
- their health plans
- family members and friends, particularly those who have therapists
- professional organizations such as a state psychological association or the National Alliance on Mental Illness (NAMI)

Often finding a good therapist involves some networking and a sequence of calls or e-mails. Norm, who has a methamphetamine addiction and PTSD, asks his aunt Beth if she can recommend a therapist. Aunt Beth recommends Carlos, who was her sister's therapist. Norm calls Carlos; Carlos explains that he doesn't have much experience working with people with drug dependence, but recommends two colleagues who do. Norm calls both. The first isn't taking new clients, but the second has openings. She explains that she has several clients with addictions, several with PTSD, and several with other co-occurring disorders. It all sounds good to Norm, so he makes an appointment, and their therapeutic relationship begins.

When seeking a referral, just saying "I've got co-occurring disorders" isn't enough. Give plenty of specific details to the person or professional who is helping you find a referral. For example: "I've got _____ (alcoholism and depression, meth addiction and PTSD, etc.). I'm hoping to find someone who specializes in my combination of disorders—or, if that isn't possible, someone who specializes in co-occurring disorders in general. My ideal therapist would also _____ (speak Spanish, be gay or lesbian, use dialectical behavior therapy, etc.)."

The Web can be a source for finding a therapist. Googling *therapist,* plus the state or metropolitan area, plus *co-occurring disorders* or *dual disorders* or *dual diagnosis,* should bring up a few therapists' names. Another option: google *therapist,* plus the relevant mental health disorder, plus the relevant substance use disorder. Clients looking for a therapist who uses a particular approach—rational emotive behavior therapy, for example—should google that plus *therapist.* However, also ask for references, and check with your state's medical licensing board before seeing someone you found online.

Getting some therapists' names and phone numbers is only the first step, of course. The next step is to call and say something like this: "Hi. My name is _____. I think I've got a mental health and substance use disorder. Your name came up as a therapist who might be right for me. Do you have a few minutes, either now or later, when we can ask each other some questions and explore whether I should make a therapy appointment with you?"

Here are some good questions to ask the therapist once he or she is available for this initial discussion:

- Are you taking new clients?
- What experience do you have working with my specific disorders? with co-occurring disorders in general? Do you have any areas of specialization?
- Do you use a particular therapeutic approach? If so, what is it?
- How long does each session last?
- Do you suggest meeting once a week at first? more often? less often?
- Do you accept the _____ health plan? (Remember, even if the therapist doesn't accept the plan, it's often possible to get reimbursed by paying the therapist's bills and submitting claims to the health plan.)
- How much will each session cost? Do you charge a sliding fee based on income?

A therapist's manner is as important as the answers they give. Someone with a pleasant manner who listens closely, and answers questions fully and directly, is worth considering—especially if they have the appropriate experience or approach. You may also prefer someone who shares your sense of humor. But someone who is distracted, angry, upset, or impatient is not likely to do good one-to-one work.

Continuing an Existing Therapeutic Relationship

What about clients who already have an ongoing relationship with a therapist? Should they continue with that therapist once they've gotten an assessment? Or should they find someone new who has a more appropriate specialty, or more experience working with co-occurring disorders?

There's no one-size-fits-all answer here. However, it's desirable to be practical and empirical. If working with a certain therapist has already yielded some genuine improvement in *both* parts of your co-occurring disorders, then it probably makes sense to stick with him or her. But if the results have been minimal, or if the therapist has helped with only one part of the disorder, then it may be better to switch to someone who has more relevant expertise. We have learned of many clients who never told their therapist about their drinking or drug use, and rationalized that it was because "they never asked." No wonder there was no improvement!

What about Group Therapy?

Group therapy (or *therapy groups* or *group counselors*) serves many of the same purposes as one-to-one therapy. However, these groups also provide a variety of benefits that one-to-one therapy cannot. As group members tell their stories and listen to those of others, they realize their situations are not as rare, as hopeless, or as shameful as they may have thought—and they feel less alone. In addition, group members support, encourage, inspire, and empathize with each other. For these reasons, group therapy is often part of nearly every formal treatment program, whether residential or outpatient, for co-occurring disorders.

But there's also a downside to group therapy: by its very nature, it can't remain focused on the specific situations and unique treatment needs of each individual. This is why most people's recovery plans often include some group therapy—as part of a formal treatment program—and some individual therapy.

Many therapists today will encourage their clients in outpatient treatment to attend Twelve Step or other peer recovery support groups. You may be strongly encouraged to attend these groups even after your therapy concludes. If you're reluctant, a therapist may explore your thoughts and attitudes about these groups in an effort to overcome your apprehensions and to motivate you to attend them. Group therapies have proven especially helpful for people with co-occurring disorders.

Group therapies sometimes involve providing the members with information. These groups are knowledge-based so clients can learn about their problems, the causes, and the recommended treatments. A second kind of group therapy focuses on teaching clients new skills. Most cognitive-behavioral therapy groups are skill-based. A third type of group therapy is called a "process" group. Process groups can be fairly open but tend to focus on "hot" issues individual members wish to share. The group therapist in a process group tries to use the group so that members help and learn from one another. Many group therapies blend knowledge, skill, and process. Some therapies focus on specific co-occurring disorders (e.g., PTSD and addiction) whereas others are like a one-room schoolhouse: the therapist works with all comers, regardless of disorders (only motivation and attendance are required).

You may also have heard about or experienced self-help groups. These independent peer recovery support groups, known as fellowships, encourage and support recovery from addictions of all types. The major Twelve Step groups include Alcoholics Anonymous, Al-Anon (for the families of alcoholics), and Narcotics Anonymous. Twelve Step groups meet regularly, have no formal leaders, and are free and open to everyone. Anonymity is an essential element of all Twelve Step groups; participants give only their first names. The Twelve Step groups Dual Recovery Anonymous, Dual Diagnosis Anonymous, and Double Trouble in Recovery are designed specifically for people with co-occurring disorders.

In these last three chapters, we've looked at the individual components that can support and encourage healing and recovery. Next, in chapter 6, we'll look at how to put these components together to create an ideal, integrated recovery plan.

CHAPTER 6

Creating a Recovery Plan

What Is a Recovery Plan?

A *recovery plan* or *treatment plan* is a map of a client's proposed journey of healing. It offers an honest look at where the client is right now, a clear statement of where the client wants to be, and specific steps and activities for getting there.

If Lionel wants to go from Chicago to New York, he doesn't just start walking east. He needs a plan. He can make a plane reservation, or get on a bus or train, or gas up his motorcycle and start riding. He can rent a car. He can go online and check out some ride-sharing bulletin boards. Or he can fly to Philadelphia, where he has some good friends, and take a train from there.

Of course, some choices are better than others. He's not going to walk. It's December, so he's not going to ride his motorcycle. He considers his options carefully, then decides to book a flight from O'Hare to Kennedy that leaves the next day.

The next morning, he packs a suitcase and takes the El to O'Hare. But when he gets there, he learns that his flight has been cancelled and the airline has rebooked him on a flight out of Midway two hours later. So Lionel takes a cab to Midway, gets on the flight, and lands at LaGuardia that afternoon. His trip hasn't gone exactly according to plan, but he's made it to New York when he wanted to, so he's happy.

We can look at Lionel's journey as a metaphor for a recovery plan. It needs to be built around the client's unique needs and circumstances. It needs to be based not on wishes or hopes, but on available and affordable options that actually work. It needs to clearly and specifically explain what the client will do and which specific professionals the client will work with. It needs to state explicitly where the client wants to go and needs to help the client get there. The plan also needs to be flexible enough to adapt to unexpected events, unforeseeable changes, even relapses.

It helps if a recovery plan is written down so clients can regularly review their goals and remind themselves of what they need to do to reach them. In fact, if you are in a formal treatment program, this document is required.

Because recovery plans are tailored to each client's disorders, needs, and personal situation, they can range from simple to highly detailed, and from informal to very formal. Let's look at both ends of this spectrum.

Chuck, who has been diagnosed with major depressive disorder, has begun drinking too much this past year. He and his therapist have put together a very simple recovery plan. It outlines Chuck's treatment: antidepressant medication and weekly talk therapy for three months, when he and his therapist will discuss next steps. It states Chuck's goals: to get and stay sober, sleep no more than nine hours a day, and get his energy and motivation up to 90 percent of their usual levels, all within the next ninety days. And it specifies what Chuck will do: take his medications as prescribed, do the homework the therapist assigns, meet with his therapist weekly, say no to his friends and colleagues who invite him out for drinks, exercise for at least half an hour a day, and attend a Twelve Step meeting at least once a week.

Because Chuck's recovery plan is simple, the written version is a simple checklist that Chuck's therapist wrote on a legal pad during Chuck's second therapy appointment. The therapist photocopied the plan for Chuck to take home.

Now, let's consider a twenty-five-year-old female. Missy has bipolar disorder, post-traumatic stress disorder, and an amphetamine (meth) disorder. She has just started a formal inpatient treatment program. Figure 6.1 shows the comprehensive recovery plan that she and the program's team of professionals created for each of her disorders. The goals in the substance use section are based on criteria developed by the American Society of Addiction Medicine. The goals in the psychiatric disorder section are taken from the Hazelden Co-occurring Disorders Program. Interventions, staff members, and frequency of meetings are listed hypothetically, as if Missy were in a hospital kind of setting.

Figure 6.1

Comprehensive Recovery Plan

Name: Missy Mills
Date of admission: 1/28/10
Date of assessment: 1/29/10
Date of current plan: 1/30/10
Substance use disorder: amphetamine dependence
Psychiatric disorders: 1. bipolar disorder 2. PTSD

Substance Use Section of Comprehensive Plan: Amphetamine Dependence

Goal	Objective	Intervention	Responsible Staff Member	Target Date
Intoxication/ withdrawal	Already detoxed—no withdrawal	Monitor	Nursing staff (Darlene Hill, primary)	Ongoing
Biomedical conditions/ complications	Hypertension (mild)	Monitor twice daily	Nursing staff (Darlene Hill, primary)	Ongoing
Emotional, behavioral, cognitive conditions/ complications	See psychiatric disorder section on pp. 2–3.			
Treatment acceptance and readiness	Enhance and solidify motivation	Motivation enhancement therapy (MET) for co-occurring disorders, individual and group	Charu Singh	2/7/10
Relapse/ continued use potential	Develop coping skills to reduce risk	Cognitive-behavioral therapy (CBT) for co-occurring disorders, individual and group	Mary Ziker	2/28/10
Recovery environment	Change existing supports; develop new supports	Twelve Step facilitation (TSF) for co-occurring disorders, individual and group	Cedric Cleary	3/15/10

continued

Figure 6.1 (cont'd)

Page 2

Psychiatric Disorder Section of Comprehensive Plan
Name: Missy Mills
Date of admission: 1/28/10

Part 1: Bipolar Disorder

Goal	Objective	Intervention	Responsible Staff Member	Target Date
Stabilize and initiate treatment	Ongoing monitoring for diagnostic accuracy	Weekly assessment	Dr. Berg	
	Client education	Client education group	Mary Ziker	2/28/10
	Enhance and solidify motivation	Motivational enhancement therapy (MET) (see p. 1)	Charu Singh	2/28/10
	Coping skills	Cognitive-behavioral therapy (CBT) for co-occurring disorders (see p. 1)	Mary Ziker	2/7/10
	Illness management and recovery skills	Twelve Step facilitation (TSF) for co-occurring disorders (see p. 1)	Cedric Cleary	2/28/10
	Symptom management	Medication management—continued on Depakote	Dr. Berg	3/15/10
	Family and social support	Family co-occurring disorders education group	Charu Singh	2/28/10

continued

Figure 6.1 (cont'd)

Page 3

Psychiatric Disorder Section of Comprehensive Plan
Name: Missy Mills
Date of admission: 1/28/10

Part 2: PTSD

Goal	Objective	Intervention	Responsible Staff Member	Target Date
Stabilize and initiate treatment	Client education	Client education group (see p. 2)	Mary Ziker	2/28/10
	Enhance and solidify motivation	Motivational enhancement therapy (MET) (see p. 1)	Charu Singh	2/28/10
	Coping skills	Cognitive-behavioral therapy (CBT) for co-occurring disorders (see p. 1)	Mary Ziker	2/7/10
	PTSD-specific symptom management	One-to-one cognitive-behavioral therapy (CBT)	Dr. King	2/28/10
	Illness management and recovery skills	Twelve Step facilitation (TSF) for co-occurring disorders (see p. 1)	Cedric Cleary	3/15/10
	Family and social support	Family co-occurring disorders education group (see p. 2)	Charu Singh	2/28/10

Notes:
After completion of the inpatient program, Missy should continue the following on an outpatient basis:
- Medication management (Dr. Berg), monthly, then tapering frequency of sessions
- One-to-one CBT (Dr. King), weekly for one month
- Twelve Step group (Cedric Cleary), three times weekly for two months

Thereafter:
- Recovery checkups (Dr. King), quarterly for one year, then annually
- Medication management (Dr. Berg), as appropriate, but at least annually
- Twelve Step meetings in the community, at least weekly

As you can see, Missy's inpatient treatment plan is more complicated than Chuck's. Missy may eventually have a simpler program once she's at home, going to work, and participating in her family routines.

At any point in recovery, clients should be able to look at their plan as a road map and say, "Here's where I am now. Here's where I'm going. Here's what I'll do next to get there. And here's what's coming up a little farther along the road." The plan should enable them to realize how far they've come, see where they've had the most success and the most difficulty, and know what payoffs and challenges await them in the future.

Depending on the client's disorders, types of treatment, and physical and mental health, a recovery plan can be as brief as ninety days or as long as a lifetime. Most recovery or aftercare plans last at least six to twelve months. For Missy and Chuck, like others with dual disorders, recovery is ongoing, of course, since each new moment requires new decisions and new actions. There's never a point where Missy might say, "I'm better now, so my recovery's over," any more than she could say, "I've reached my weight-loss goal, so now I can pig out as much and as often as I want."

Who Creates a Recovery Plan?

A recovery plan can be created in any of three ways:

1. Using the traditional hierarchical approach, in which a professional alone, without a real alliance with the client, creates a recovery plan for the client and advises (or orders) him or her to follow it. In this model, the professional can easily overlook or ignore the client's legitimate needs, preferences, or experience. This reduces trust, compliance, and the likelihood that the treatment will work.

2. Using the consumerist approach, in which a professional provides information to the client and suggests the client collect additional information on his or her own. The client then designs the recovery plan, perhaps with the professional's input. In this model, the client can easily make poor decisions because of limited knowledge and experience, and the professional is very "hands-off."

3. Using the shared decision-making approach, in which the professional and the client form an alliance and work together to create a recovery plan, combining the professional's knowledge and experience of the client's stage of motivation with the client's awareness of his or her own body, psyche, emotions, situation, and needs.

For the great majority of co-occurring disorders, my colleagues and I at the Dartmouth Medical School strongly recommend the shared decision-making model. This model is also recommended for making most important health care and recovery decisions.

Modern health care is based on three essential components: (1) current scientific information, (2) client preferences, and (3) professionals' skills. Shared decision making based on the client's stage of change and motivation brings these three components together. By sharing their expertise with each other, the professional and client can negotiate a plan that is most likely to succeed.

Shared decision making encourages—and, in fact, requires—clients to take responsibility for their treatment and recovery. And it helps to form a stronger, more trusting, and more collaborative relationship between the client and the professional.

Are there situations in which shared decision making isn't wise? Certainly. When a disorder is so severe that clients can't think properly, are at severe suicidal risk, or can't control their behavior, then it is up to a professional to temporarily take over and make decisions for them. However, these decisions should all be geared toward stabilizing the clients' condition and restoring their ability to think and make decisions on their own. Once this has been achieved, the professional needs to let go of absolute control; the professional and the client can then work together to create a recovery plan.

This chapter has spoken repeatedly of "the professional." But just who is this person? The professional who conducts the assessment? The therapist the client chooses to work with? A professional at the formal treatment program the client selects?

In practice, it can be any of these people—or some combination. Let's look at how treatment plans for three different people were created.

> When Larry sat down to discuss his assessment results with a therapist—a nurse practitioner—he liked her immediately. Her diagnosis of dysthymia and marijuana dependence felt right. She seemed knowledgeable but not stuffy, and she wasn't in a hurry. Best of all, she seemed to really understand what he was feeling and going through. She empathized, and didn't seem to argue or oppose his ideas of what was wrong.
>
> When the therapist suggested an antidepressant plus one-to-one therapy with her, Larry quickly agreed. At his next appointment with her, they created his recovery plan together.
>
> Anton was shocked and surprised when the psychiatrist told him that he had both generalized anxiety disorder and cocaine dependence. But he also knew

that his life was getting more difficult and painful—and more expensive—
every day. He told the psychiatrist that he was eager to recover. The doctor
recommended that he begin with a formal treatment program and gave him a list
of three integrated programs at sites in the area. But Anton didn't want to begin
his recovery in Tucson in the summer, so he looked into several programs in the
Pacific Northwest. He found one he liked near Seattle. Soon after he arrived, he
and a program therapist put together his recovery plan.

Leah cried when the psychologist told her, "We both know you've got an
OxyContin addiction. But you've also got major depression, and the combina-
tion of the two can be deadly. I'm really glad you got assessed when you did.
You might have just saved your own life."

Leah wiped away the tears and said, "Okay. What do you think I should do
next?" The psychologist recommended an aggressive combination of medication,
a formal treatment program, and one-to-one therapy. Leah nodded. "All right.
Will you work with me?"

The therapist shook his head. "I can't; I'll be out of the country most of the
fall. But let me give you the names of three of my colleagues who deal with co-
occurring disorders. I also recommend you talk with Darcy, who works in our
mental health clinic here at our treatment program. We've got a new outpatient
program starting in about two weeks, and there may still be some space in it.
And let me also give you the name and phone number of a very good psychiatrist
here at the clinic. She's the one who can initially prescribe your meds."

A week later, Leah began one-to-one therapy with one of the recommended
therapists. A week after that, she also began outpatient treatment at the clinic.
Working as a team, four people put together Leah's treatment plan: her therapist, a psychologist and a psychiatrist from the treatment program, and Leah
herself.

Recovery and Real Life

No recovery plan is written in stone. As clients grow, learn, and change, their plans
may need to change as well. Dates may be moved ahead or back. Treatment may be
extended, ended earlier, or changed. Medications may be altered, added, or removed.
Because recovery is a dynamic process, any recovery plan must be a living document—

and both the client and the professionals working with the client must be willing to say, when necessary, "Let's revisit the recovery plan."

Of course, even an ideal recovery plan won't work if the client doesn't follow it. That's why the two most important elements of recovery are the client's courage to change and willingness to step into a new and unfamiliar life.

Let's take a closer look at where courage and willingness come from, and at how change begins.

CHAPTER 7

The Courage to Change

Even the best treatment plan, and the earnest efforts of talented professionals, can't have much effect unless the client is willing to change or at least is open to the possibility. Individuals in recovery from co-occurring disorders eventually have to face the same truth: positive change in their lives starts with them. This means doing some things they're not used to—things that at first might seem awkward or scary or unnatural.

Change takes courage—a willingness to move forward into what's unfamiliar or unknown, in spite of our fear. Yet there are two even more powerful motivators than courage: a deep dissatisfaction with what our lives have become, and our sincere desire for recovery and serenity.

In this chapter, we'll look closely at the stages, benefits, and challenges of change. You will be asked to think on and answer some questions about yourself. Some questions will require written answers, and worksheets have been provided for you to fill in. Rather than writing directly in this book, photocopy pages 73, 76, 85, 108, and 111 and write on the photocopies. You'll need to make multiple copies of the forms on pages 78, 82, 103, 157, and 159. (You can also download full-page versions of these worksheets at www.cooccurring.org.)

The question-and-answer process in this chapter will give you a taste of the early stages of recovery. However, this book is not intended as treatment or therapy, and it is not meant to replace the services of qualified professionals, treatment programs, and/or support groups. Its goal is to introduce, explain, and augment these services, not replace them.

This chapter uses a number of techniques adapted from motivational enhancement therapy (MET). As you'll soon see, chapters 8 and 9 introduce and adapt certain techniques from cognitive-behavioral therapy (CBT), and chapter 10 examines and discusses Twelve Step programs. These three components—MET, CBT, and TSF (Twelve Step facilitation)—form the Co-occurring Disorders Program, a widely used model developed by faculty from the Dartmouth Medical School.

Start Where You Are

In order to plan and begin any journey, it's essential to know exactly where you are right now.

So, using worksheet 7.1 on page 73, take a look at your life, note the things you're happy about, and identify the ones you're unhappy about. This exercise should be completed in three steps.

> *Step 1.* Look at the column headed "Aspect" on worksheet 7.1. For each aspect of your life on this list, circle a number from 1 to 9; a 1 means you're completely dissatisfied, and a 9 means you're completely satisfied. This will take about three to six minutes. Complete this task before reading on.

1 = Completely dissatisfied
2 = Mostly dissatisfied
3 = Somewhat dissatisfied
4 = Slightly dissatisfied
5 = Neutral
6 = Slightly satisfied
7 = Somewhat satisfied
8 = Mostly satisfied
9 = Completely satisfied

Worksheet 7.1

My Life Evaluation

Aspect	Rating	Link	Change
Friends and social life	1 2 3 4 5 6 7 8 9		
Job/work	1 2 3 4 5 6 7 8 9		
Where I live	1 2 3 4 5 6 7 8 9		
Money and financial security	1 2 3 4 5 6 7 8 9		
Education and learning	1 2 3 4 5 6 7 8 9		
Leisure time and fun	1 2 3 4 5 6 7 8 9		
Mood and self-esteem	1 2 3 4 5 6 7 8 9		
Anger and arguments	1 2 3 4 5 6 7 8 9		
Stress and anxiety	1 2 3 4 5 6 7 8 9		
Physical health	1 2 3 4 5 6 7 8 9		
Spirituality	1 2 3 4 5 6 7 8 9		
Love and affection	1 2 3 4 5 6 7 8 9		
Family relationships*	1 2 3 4 5 6 7 8 9		
Relationship with my spouse or partner**	1 2 3 4 5 6 7 8 9		
Sexuality	1 2 3 4 5 6 7 8 9		
Eating and weight	1 2 3 4 5 6 7 8 9		
Physical activity and exercise	1 2 3 4 5 6 7 8 9		
Giving/caring for others	1 2 3 4 5 6 7 8 9		
Mental ability, memory	1 2 3 4 5 6 7 8 9		
Personal safety, security	1 2 3 4 5 6 7 8 9		

* If you don't have any living family members, skip this line.

** If you don't have a spouse or partner, skip this line.

Step 2. Now, once you've circled a number for each aspect of your life, go back to the top of the chart. Carefully consider whether each aspect has been affected by your mental health problem, your substance use problem, or both. In the column headed "Link," write MH (if the aspect has been affected by your mental health disorder), SU (if it has been affected by your substance use disorder), B (if it has been affected by both), or nothing at all (if neither one affects it). For example, for the first aspect, "Friends and social life," you might write B (affected by both your substance use and mental health) under Link. This step usually takes about five to ten minutes.

Step 3. Go down the list one last time. This time, under the column headed Change, put a check next to each part of your life that you would like to see changed or improved. For aspects you don't want to change at all, leave the Change column blank. For most people, this step takes only two to five minutes.

When you fill in this worksheet—or any of the worksheets in this book—it helps to be in a quiet place, free from distractions. Because these forms require honest reflection and introspection, it's also best to work on them when you aren't feeling stressed or hurried.

Although most of these worksheets can be completed quickly, a few require half an hour or more.

When you've completed worksheet 7.1, sit back and look over what you've done. You've just painted a detailed picture of your own current level of satisfaction. At a glance, you can tell what you feel good about in your life and what you don't.

The areas where you feel mostly or completely satisfied probably don't require you to change. Those where you feel dissatisfied or neutral, however, are not likely to improve much until *you* change.

Post this chart in a place where you'll see it often. This has two purposes: first, as a reminder of what areas in your life may need attention; and, second, as a baseline against which to compare new information in the future, as your recovery proceeds.

Now you're going to give some depth to the picture by identifying some specific problems in your life.

On worksheet 7.2 on page 76, list ten to twenty of the problems in your life, in any order you like. Include all of the largest, most chronic, and most bothersome ones, plus any others you're concerned about. You don't have to come up with twenty, but list at least ten.

One way to approach this task is to look back at worksheet 7.1. For each aspect of your life where you feel dissatisfied or neutral, ask yourself, *What problem or problems keep me from feeling satisfied about this part of my life?* For example, if you gave "Spirituality" a rank of 3 (somewhat dissatisfied), you might identify your specific problem as "Finding a congregation where I feel at home." Or, if you gave "Eating and weight" a rank of 2 (mostly dissatisfied), you might note your problem as "Eating too much, especially sugar, when I'm stressed out."

Worksheet 7.2 requires some serious thought and reflection—so it typically takes thirty to sixty minutes to fill out.

When you're done, look over your list. If you like, in the left column, number the problems from most to least troubling.

Post this list next to your satisfaction/dissatisfaction rankings. Together, these two pages will give you a clear view of what you're happy with in your life, what you're not happy with, and what specific problems you most need to address.

Now it's time to look at the process of change itself.

Worksheet 7.2

My Life Problems

_____ Problem: _____

_____ Problem: _____

_____ Problem: _____

_____ Problem: _____

_____ Problem: _____

_____ Problem: _____

_____ Problem: _____

_____ Problem: _____

_____ Problem: _____

_____ Problem: _____

_____ Problem: _____

_____ Problem: _____

_____ Problem: _____

_____ Problem: _____

_____ Problem: _____

_____ Problem: _____

_____ Problem: _____

_____ Problem: _____

_____ Problem: _____

_____ Problem: _____

The Case for Change

We've already noted that willingness is a basic requirement for making any real, long-lasting change. Yet willingness is actually a lifeline made up of three intertwined strands: *importance, confidence,* and *readiness.* Someone contemplating a change isn't going to go through with it unless (1) they consider the change important; (2) they're reasonably confident that they can make the change; and (3) they're ready to make the change.

With this in mind, take a closer look at some of the problems you might address—and some of the changes you might make—in your recovery.

Make ten to twenty photocopies of worksheet 7.3 on page 78—one for each of the problems you listed in worksheet 7.2. (Or you can download a full-page version of this worksheet at www.cooccurring.org.) Write one problem on each photocopy. *For each separate problem,* use the scales provided to indicate how important it is for you to address this problem; how confident you feel in being able to address the problem (provided you can get others' help and support); and how ready you are to change the problem.

Circle whatever numbers feel right. If you want to put a circle in between two numbers, that's fine. Don't worry that you might feel otherwise a week, a day, or an hour from now. Just make your best judgment based on how you feel right now.

It will probably take one to three minutes to complete a form for each problem.

My Willingness to Change

Problem: _____

Importance

1	2	3	4	5	6	7	8	9
Not at all important		Somewhat important		Fairly important		Very important		Extremely important

Confidence

1	2	3	4	5	6	7	8	9
Not at all confident		Somewhat confident		Fairly confident		Very confident		Extremely confident

Readiness

1	2	3	4	5	6	7	8	9
Not at all ready		Somewhat ready		Fairly ready		Very ready		Extremely ready

When you've finished, spend a few minutes looking over all your Willingness to Change forms. The problems for which you circled high numbers (a 6 or above in all three sections) may be the most ripe for addressing early in your recovery.

Look over these problem evaluations carefully. Then keep them in a place where you can easily find and review them as your recovery moves forward.

Changing What You Can

One common mistake people make, especially early in their recovery, is trying to change things they can't. This only creates wasted effort and frustration.

It's important instead to focus your efforts on things you *can* change. Figure 7.1 shows the difference.

Figure 7.1

Changing What You Can

Things You *Can't* Change, No Matter How Hard You Try	Things You *Can* Change
Other people	Yourself
The past	Your direction in life now
Your feelings right now	Your thoughts and attitudes about your feelings
Your circumstances right now	Your present direction and attitude

The famous Serenity Prayer is based on this important distinction:

God, grant me the serenity
To accept the things I cannot change,
The courage to change the things I can,
And the wisdom to know the difference.

Weighing Your Options

The next task is to evaluate (1) the benefits of not changing, (2) the drawbacks or consequences of not changing, and (3) the benefits of making a change. Here's an example. Jimmy has trouble sleeping more than a few hours a night, mostly because of his cocaine use. But Jimmy gets some benefits from this situation:

- He can spend more time surfing the Web late at night.
- He can watch more late-night TV.
- He doesn't have to put any effort into changing his life.
- His sleepiness and his late-night activities are familiar and predictable. They're almost like old friends.

But there are also some clear drawbacks to not sleeping enough:

- He's tired most of the time.
- He has trouble concentrating. He almost caused two auto accidents last month.
- His job performance is slipping. Because he's a salesman on commission, his earnings are down almost 15 percent.
- He doesn't exercise as much as he would like, because he just doesn't have the energy.

Jimmy craves cocaine more often because it boosts his sense of himself. He realizes that if he were able to sleep seven or eight hours a night, he would

- feel better
- have more energy
- exercise more, which, in turn, would give him still more energy
- concentrate better
- improve his performance at work—and make more money
- be a safer driver, and possibly spare himself an accident

Here's another example: one of Amina's problems is that her sister Sabina regularly humiliates her—especially about her job as a waitress—in front of their family. (Amina has a master's degree, and Sabina regularly berates her for not using it.) Amina knows she can't change what her sister feels or thinks or does. Here are some things she *can* do, however:

- Before the next family event, she can tell Sabina how much it hurts when she criticizes her in front of their family. Sabina can then decide for herself how to treat Amina at future family gatherings.

- Before the next family event, Amina can tell Sabina that if she starts picking on her, even a little, she'll leave. If Sabina does start humiliating her at the event, Amina can thank everyone else and leave quickly.
- She can ask other family members to stick up for her when Sabina criticizes her.
- She can avoid Sabina as much as possible at family gatherings.
- She can skip family gatherings when she knows Sabina will be there.
- She can bring a large feather to family gatherings. If Sabina starts criticizing her, she can tickle her sister with it until she stops. (If she doesn't stop, Amina can leave.)

Amina can also look for a more high-powered job, of course. But she should only do this if that's something she wants for herself. Taking a different job just to get her sister off her back only strengthens Sabina's power over her. And if Amina does get a more intellectual job, her sister may still criticize her.

Now it's time for you to do your own cost-benefit analysis using worksheet 7.4 on page 82. As before, make multiple photocopies of the worksheet—one for each of the problems you listed in worksheet 7.2. (Or you can download a full-page version of this worksheet at www.cooccurring.org.) Use a separate copy for each problem. List the problem, then evaluate it under the three headings.

You'll probably need to spend five to ten minutes on each problem.

There are seven spaces under each heading, but you don't have to write down exactly seven responses. After you've thought seriously about a problem, write in however many responses you come up with.

Remember that it's important to focus on what you *can* change, not on what you would *like* to change but can't change.

Worksheet 7.4

Costs and Benefits of Changing

Problem: _____

	Reasons Not to Change (Benefits of continuing to have this problem)	Reasons to Change, Part 1 (Drawbacks of continuing to have this problem)	Reasons to Change, Part 2 (Benefits of no longer having this problem)
1.			
2.			
3.			
4.			
5.			
6.			
7.			

Review your completed forms carefully, and then save them in an easily accessible spot. As your recovery progresses, you can periodically look them over and realize how much progress you've made.

Stages of Change

Psychologists have conceptualized and observed that people go through four common stages whenever they make a change in their lives. This is called the four-stage model of change:*

- *Stage 1: Precontemplation.* The person either sees no reason to change or has no interest in changing. They may never have thought about changing. Or they may have (or think they have) good reasons to stay the way they are. Someone who says, "I don't have a problem" or "Problem? What problem?" is in stage 1.
- *Stage 2: Contemplation.* The person is seriously considering changing, but isn't sure it's a good idea or has mixed feelings about it. They can see both the pluses and the minuses of changing. They can also see the pluses and minuses of *not* changing. Someone who says, "Something's not right, but I'm not sure what it is or what to do about it" or "I might have a problem, and I may need to do something about it" is in stage 2.
- *Stage 3: Action.* The person has decided that change is a good idea and has begun to make that change. Someone who says, "I need to deal with this, so here's what I'm going to do first" or "I'm going to make a plan for change and figure out some steps and strategies" is in stage 3.
- *Stage 4: Maintenance.* The person has already changed. They've stopped drinking or drugging, or ended a harmful relationship, or stabilized their mental health through medications and lifestyle changes. Now they need to focus their efforts on not relapsing or reverting back. Someone who says, "I did it, but now I need to make it stick" or "I'm where I want to be, but now I need support and a plan to help me stay there" is in stage 4.

To complete your 360-degree view of your life as it is right now, take each of the ten to twenty problems you identified earlier and list them on worksheet 7.5 on page 85. (It's

---

* The stages presented here are adapted from J. O. Prochaska, J. C. Norcross, and C. C. DiClemente, *Changing for Good: A Revolutionary Six-Stage Program for Overcoming Bad Habits and Moving Your Life Positively Forward* (New York: William Morrow and Company, 1994).

okay if you don't have ten to twenty problems to list.) For each problem, indicate what stage of change you're in and how you know you're in this stage. Depending on how many problems you've listed, this worksheet usually takes between fifteen and forty-five minutes to complete. If you need more time, however, feel free to take it.

Worksheet 7.5

Stages of Change

1. List each problem in the appropriate space.
2. Write what stage of change best describes where you are right now. This will be a number between 1 and 4. (Don't worry about doing this perfectly. Just write the number that seems the most accurate as of this moment.)
3. To the right of that number, write down how you know you're in this stage. In other words, write down what you've noticed yourself do, feel, or think that tells you that this is the stage you're in with that problem.

Problem	Stage	Evidence That I'm in This Stage
1. _____	_____	_____
2. _____	_____	_____
3. _____	_____	_____
4. _____	_____	_____
5. _____	_____	_____
6. _____	_____	_____
7. _____	_____	_____
8. _____	_____	_____
9. _____	_____	_____
10. _____	_____	_____
11. _____	_____	_____
12. _____	_____	_____
13. _____	_____	_____
14. _____	_____	_____
15. _____	_____	_____
16. _____	_____	_____
17. _____	_____	_____
18. _____	_____	_____
19. _____	_____	_____
20. _____	_____	_____

Moving Forward

Congratulations! You've painted a clear, detailed portrait of your life as it is right now—including its benefits and drawbacks; how you feel about each aspect of it; which aspects you're ready and willing to address; and which ones you're most hesitant to deal with right now.

The rest of this book will help you make and maintain changes that can improve your life, promote your recovery and healing, and lead to greater happiness and serenity.

To take the next step forward into recovery and healing, turn the page.

CHAPTER 8

Pervasive Benefits of Cognitive-Behavioral Therapy

The Case for Cognitive-Behavioral Therapy (CBT)

Cognitive-behavioral therapy (CBT) has an excellent track record of reducing negativity, anxiety, distress, irritability, and physical tension. In addition, PET scans have confirmed that CBT enables people to make beneficial physical changes in their brains. But what makes CBT especially valuable is its ability to help people create more positive and realistic ways of thinking, feeling, and acting. In the *Forbes* article "Patient Fix Thyself" (April 9, 2007), writer Robert Langreth observed, "CBT drops the endless search for past hurts, teaches patients how to prevent negative thoughts from creeping into their minds and coaches them on how to cope."

Perhaps with its roots as far back as Norman Vincent Peale's *The Power of Positive Thinking*, CBT has proven particularly effective in treating co-occurring disorders, especially when combined with appropriate medication. Unlike improvements resulting from medication alone, which typically end when the person stops taking the medication, gains made through CBT tend to be sustained even after therapy ends. That is to say, most people who master basic CBT skills continue to improve long after their formal treatment is complete.

This chapter and chapter 9 introduce CBT and show you how to use its most beneficial tools, concepts, and techniques. You'll be able quickly to put these to practical use in your own life.

If you're in a formal treatment program or one-to-one CBT, the material presented here and in earlier chapters will echo and augment what you'll encounter in treatment. If you're not, remember that this book is not meant to replace a treatment program or one-to-one therapy.

What Is Cognitive-Behavioral Therapy?

Cognitive-behavioral therapy is one of many general *therapeutic approaches*—that is, forms of psychotherapy. CBT itself has many variations, such as rational emotive behavior therapy, problem-solving therapy, cognitive therapy, reality therapy, and dialectical behavior therapy. However, all forms of CBT share these characteristics:

- CBT focuses on the here and now, not on what happened in the past.
- CBT involves learning new skills. In CBT, people don't just talk about whatever comes to mind. They learn new ways of thinking that help them reduce anxiety and relax in stressful situations; new skills for managing difficult or painful feelings and situations; and new ways to process their thoughts and experiences so that new ways of feeling and acting can emerge.
- CBT skills require regular practice. The more someone practices these skills in their daily life, the better they get at using them, and the more solid and sustained their recovery is likely to be.
- In CBT, treatment ends after a limited time: usually thirty to ninety days in a formal treatment program, and two to six months (ten to twenty-five sessions) in one-to-one therapy, though some people may need as much as a year. Sometimes booster sessions or checkups are a good idea. But CBT is typically time-limited and focused on your becoming your own therapist. It is like teaching people to fish instead of giving them fish.

CBT is based on an awareness that our thoughts and our interpretations of situations create many of our negative and positive feelings. Put more simply, how we think often creates how we feel. CBT teaches people to be aware of their thinking styles, analyze whether those styles are realistic or helpful, and, when appropriate, replace them with new, more beneficial, and more accurate ways of thinking.

Many people with mental health and substance use disorders regularly experience a cascade of irrational fears, worries, and other unrealistically negative thoughts. These then create negative feelings—anger, shame, anxiety, fear, sadness, despair—which in turn lead to potential harmful actions, from isolation to drinking and drugging to violence to risky sexual behavior. Obviously, if you have substance use and mental health disorders, these negative thoughts and beliefs will seriously undermine your recovery.

CBT helps people see how they tend to think in certain predictable but inaccurate ways, which therapists call *cognitive distortions* or *cognitive styles*. (They also go by some far less technical names, including *common thinking errors, common styles of thinking,* and *stinking thinking*.) CBT helps people to see how these styles, distortions, or errors can lead to unwarranted harmful actions and distressing emotions.

Through CBT, people discover that they have far more power to change their thoughts, feelings, and actions than they ever imagined. They literally learn to reconsider their automatic thoughts and more flexibly access hope, joy, excitement, empathy, and inspiration.

The process works like this. One evening, Alitha works late. She hurries to the train station but just misses the last commuter train of the day. Because of her mental health disorder, Alitha tends toward "worst case scenario" thinking: she imagines that terrible, unavoidable things will happen because she missed the train. She probably will be attacked and robbed. She worries about what will happen when she gets home very late: her husband will shout at her; they'll have a fight; she'll be so upset that she won't be able to get to sleep; she'll be a wreck the next day and will screw up her important presentation; she'll be called into the boss's office and fired for poor performance; her husband will be furious with her; they'll divorce; and, in a few months, she'll be broke and alone. Standing on the platform at the deserted train station, Alitha starts to sob and wonders how she managed to screw up her life so badly. She briefly considers throwing herself down onto the rails.

All that actually happened, though, is she missed her train.

Because Alitha has begun practicing CBT skills, she wipes her eyes, shakes her head at her own negativity, and considers her options. She can take a cab—no, too pricey. She can take a bus—no, she'd have to transfer at Kensington Station, and it would take her ninety minutes. She thinks for a few seconds, then nods. She knows just what to do.

She takes out her cell phone and calls her husband. "Honey, it's getting so late—let's go out for pizza instead of cooking. How about if we meet at Mario's in about thirty-five minutes?" Mario's is a block from Kensington Station. Her husband, who loves Italian food, agrees enthusiastically. As she hangs up, Alitha smiles and thinks, *I'll sleep eight hours tonight and ace the presentation tomorrow.* What did Alitha do? She stopped catastrophizing and found a creative solution!

For people with co-occurring disorders, CBT can consist of three main components: *mindful relaxation, education,* and *flexible thinking.* First, clients learn a new way of breathing that helps them reduce tension and anxiety. Next, they learn about their mental health disorder—including its symptoms, causes, and forms of treatment—and how it interacts with drugs and alcohol. Then, in flexible thinking, which is the heart of CBT, they learn new ways of processing their experience in order to create more evidence-based and more adaptive and positive ways of thinking and acting.

Mindful Relaxation

Mindful relaxation is a simple process that retrains us to naturally and physically reduce tension and anxiety. This new way of mindfulness helps people relax in stressful situations and gives them a sense of greater control over anxiety, distress, and other unpleasant feelings. It can also help them cope with cravings or pressures to use alcohol or drugs.

Virtually everyone with co-occurring disorders—and many people without co-occurring disorders—often experiences anxiety, tension, worry, and/or fear. When we feel any of these, we tend to get agitated and breathe faster—or else we start inhaling slowly and deliberately, hoping to calm ourselves down.

Researchers have learned through many laboratory studies, though, that both of these forms of breathing *increase* anxiety rather than reduce it. Taking in more air than we need signals to our bodies that we're in danger; this, in turn, makes us more anxious. To calm down, we need to not only slow down our breathing but also take in *less* air. The key to reducing anxiety through breathing is to *inhale normally* and *exhale slowly*. It's slow *exhaling* that creates calm and relaxation, not slow inhaling.

Mindful relaxation has two main parts. Here are step-by-step instructions:

1. The first part is a "centering" or "grounding" exercise. This will help you get in touch with yourself and eliminate the noise of your busy thoughts and feelings. The idea behind centering is to help you reach a state of feeling present, stable, and in tune with yourself. This will help you benefit more from the relaxing breathing.
   - Get in as comfortable a position as you can.
   - Make sure both feet are on the ground. Press the balls of your feet onto the floor. Relax.
   - Close your eyes, breathe normally, and try to relax.
   - Visualize your center or core—the core of you. Many people locate this somewhere between their spine and belly button.
   - Drop down into this center.

- Relax, pay attention, and experience this core. Notice that it is calm, present, and yours. Notice that it balances your body—from top to bottom, from side to side. Spend two to three minutes in this relaxed state.

2. The second part is a breathing exercise. The idea behind relaxing breathing is to help you focus on the way you inhale and exhale, so that your body is more able to feel relaxed, soothed, and calm. If you breathe in too much without a full exhale, you will actually feel more anxiety and arousal. However, if you balance the way you breathe in and out, you will feel much better.
   - Pay attention to your breathing.
   - Take a normal breath in through your nose.
   - As you exhale, try to extend your breathing out through your mouth. Don't do it so that it is uncomfortable, but just a little longer than you had been doing.
   - Try it again: normal breath in through your nose, longer breath out through your mouth.
   - Repeat the breathing until you have done ten to fifteen breaths. (Hint: You may also think of a word that calms you while you do this. This could be a word like *serene, peace,* or simply *calm.* Or if you want, picture a scene that is relaxing to you. It should be easy and make you feel safe.)

Mindful relaxation is a skill that can really help you manage anxiety, fear, and stress. But like all skills, you need to practice it to get good at it. The better you are at it, the more it will help you when you need it most. It's kind of like a fire drill—it's best to practice under normal circumstances so that it becomes automatic or reflexive. This makes success more likely during times of stress.

Practice mindful relaxation twice a day, every day, for ten to fifteen breaths when you are not feeling stressed. This will not take long at all, and doing it when nothing is upsetting you will help you get good at it. It will then be easy to use when you are anxious, scared, or panicky.

How Flexible Thinking Works

Nobody's life is free of stress or difficulties. Yet two people can have very different emotional reactions to the same source of stress. This is because the primary cause of how we feel is not *what* happens to us, but *how we think about* what happens to us.

Remember what happened when Alitha missed her train? At first she had a cascade of unpleasant—and unrealistic—thoughts that eventually led her to consider suicide. *That whole sequence of thoughts, images, and feelings was generated by her own mind.*

Then Alitha caught herself. She realized that her situation wasn't as awful as she imagined. So she contemplated her options and created a solution: meeting her husband for dinner near Kensington Station. Soon she was smiling, happy, and looking forward to dinner and to the following day. *This sequence of thoughts, images, and feelings was also generated by her own mind.* This simple fact can be difficult for many to believe. It's not unusual to be convinced that one's thoughts are true and accurate and not just coming from the mind.

People with mental health and substance use disorders typically contend with many upsetting and distressing emotions. These feelings tend to lead to unrealistically negative thoughts. When people practice flexible thinking, they identify those negative thoughts, challenge those thoughts by evaluating the evidence for and against them, and replace those thoughts with more realistic, flexible, and positive ones. This improves how they feel and helps them make better decisions, whether it be a different thought or a different plan of action.

Alitha was quickly able to identify all her negative thoughts about being late: her husband's anger; the fight they would have; how upset she would feel; her inability to sleep; her poor performance at work the next day; the meeting with her boss where she'd be fired; a bigger fight with her husband; getting divorced; being broke and alone. She realized that none of these things was actually inevitable; they took place entirely in her imagination. Then she evaluated how realistic these ideas were. Yes, her husband might be upset that she was so late, but that didn't mean they'd fight or that she'd be unable to sleep. And even if he was mad at her, that didn't mean she couldn't do anything about it. She could apologize, or buy him flowers, or put on her sexiest negligee and pull him into the bedroom.

She also realized that she didn't even have to be all that late. She considered her options and came up with dinner at Mario's. She not only solved the problem of missing the last train but also now felt happy instead of miserable.

Flexible thinking can be useful for anyone. But it's especially valuable for people with co-occurring disorders. Many people with these disorders abuse alcohol or drugs in an attempt to push aside their shame, fear, anxiety, anger, depression, insomnia, and other negative emotions and conditions. When they begin their recovery and stop drinking or drugging, those negative emotions and conditions usually come roaring back. One additional value of flexible thinking is that it helps people navigate these feelings and difficulties without having to resort to mind-altering substances.

How Thoughts Create Emotions

Imagine that Brandon sees his neighbor Tamara leaving the grocery store. He smiles and waves at her, but she doesn't smile or wave back. Instead, she quickly brushes past him, looking straight ahead.

Here are some of the thoughts Brandon could have about the encounter:

- *I wonder if I pissed her off for some reason. After supper I'll knock on her door and bring her a couple of brownies. Then I'll ask her what I did to offend her.*
- *She didn't recognize me. That's strange. I wonder if I look that different with my beard shaved off.*
- *She snubbed me. What a jerk!*
- *Jeez, it's like I'm invisible to women. Am I really that bad looking?*
- *Man, people are unfriendly in this town. Even my own neighbors won't wave hello.*

Each of these thoughts leads to a very different conclusion—and a very different emotion. Yet they're all responses to the exact same situation.

Which, if any, of these responses is correct? Brandon will never know unless he asks Tamara about it later—or unless he turns around. Fortunately, he does, just in time to see her grab a toddler that is about to run into the busy street.

Flexible thinking recognizes that our thinking often creates our mood or feelings, rather than the other way around. Figure 8.1, for example, shows how distorted thinking plays a role in creating negative emotions.

Figure 8.1

Thinking and Emotions

General Thought	Specific Thought	Emotions Caused by Those Thoughts
Something bad will happen.	I'm going to be attacked or hurt. I'm going to be rejected or abandoned or ignored. I'm going to lose control or go crazy.	Anxiety and fear
I'm going to lose.	I can't depend on anyone. I'm a loser. Nothing good ever happens to me. Life isn't worth living.	Depression and sadness
I'm bad or shameful.	When bad things happen to me, it's my fault. I'm too messed up for anyone to want me. I'm unlovable.	Shame and guilt
I'm being used or abused.	I'm being mistreated. My boss is exploiting me again. I'm a victim.	Irritability and anger

Sometimes, of course, some thoughts and feelings may be entirely appropriate. If Lincoln opens an e-mail from a friend, but it turns out to be a computer virus, he'll briefly be angry—and for good reason. Who wouldn't be angry about getting a computer virus?

Flexible thinking isn't about never feeling angry, or scared, or lonely, or sad. It's about letting go of negative thoughts *that don't apply to the situation.*

Alitha recognized that her own dire thoughts didn't accurately reflect her situation. So she dropped them and created a solution to her problem. Similarly, when Brandon turned around, he saw that his initial thought about Tamara had nothing to do with the real situation.

Figure 8.2

Taking a Reality Check

General Thought	Reality Check	Internal Response
Something bad will happen.	What specific bad thing is going to happen? How likely is it to happen? What evidence do I have that it will happen? What evidence do I have that it *won't* happen?	Anxiety or fear dissipates.
I'm going to lose.	What exactly am I going to lose? How likely is that to happen? What evidence do I have that it will happen? What evidence do I have that it *won't* happen?	Depression or sadness lifts.
I'm bad or shameful.	What bad or wrong thing did I actually do? How much harm did I actually do, and to whom? What evidence do I have that I genuinely did something wrong? What evidence do I have to the contrary?	Shame or guilt disappears.
I'm being used or abused.	What is genuinely unfair about this situation? Who has actually wronged me? What harm have I actually sustained? What evidence do I have for this? What evidence do I have to the contrary?	Irritability or anger lessens.

As shown in figure 8.2 on the previous page, flexible thinking enables people to respond to negative thoughts by asking themselves questions that serve as reality checks. Next time you have thoughts such as those in the chart, ask yourself the appropriate questions. Doing this will help you determine whether your thoughts and feelings are appropriate, or whether you've gotten stuck in a cognitive distortion.

Twelve Common Cognitive Distortions

In *Cognitive Therapy: Basics and Beyond* (The Guilford Press, 1995), Judith S. Beck describes the most common types of cognitive distortions (or stinking thinking). She calls them "distortions," but everyone uses any one or a combination of these, whether they have co-occurring disorders or not. Take a moment to become familiar with these styles, which have been adapted from Beck's work and are shown in figure 8.3.

Figure 8.3

Twelve Common Cognitive Distortions

Tunnel vision	Focuses only on the negative characteristics of something, not the positive ones.	"My boss is awful. She's demanding, judgmental, and opinionated." "My life is terrible. Nothing is going well."
All-or-nothing thinking (black-and-white, polarized, or dichotomous thinking)	Looks at things as falling into only two extreme categories ("black or white") instead of on a continuum ("shades of gray").	"My neighborhood isn't totally safe, therefore it's extremely dangerous." "If I'm not perfect, I'm a total failure."
"Should" and "must" statements (imperatives)	Are based on predetermined ideas about how things are supposed to be, not on how things really are or could reasonably be.	"I should be more willing to take risks." "I must stop feeling afraid all the time." "I shouldn't make mistakes."

continued

Worst case scenario thinking	Predicts that the absolute worst, most awful outcome will happen. This can make a small problem seem like it will turn into a catastrophe.	"What if someone breaks into my house and rapes me?!" "What if I yell at my son and he hates me forever?!"
Personalization	Leads you to believe that you're responsible for things that are actually out of your control, such as how others behave, think, or feel.	"My therapist was late because I said the wrong thing last week." "My husband only hits me when I'm a bad wife."
Disqualifying or discounting the positive	Leads you to minimize or downplay positive events because you believe they don't count (anyone could do it, you got lucky, or it wasn't *that* good).	"I've been sober for a week, but anyone can last a week." "I passed my certification, but it was just dumb luck."
Overgeneralization	Takes a single distressing situation and concludes that it will continue in a never-ending pattern, and will probably get worse.	"That man raped me; men will always take advantage of me." "I had a bad dream. I'll never get a good night's sleep."
Emotional reasoning	Assumes that because you *feel* a certain way, that's how it must *be* in reality.	"I am scared, therefore something bad is about to happen." "I feel angry, so obviously you have treated me terribly."
Mind reading	Happens when you believe you know what someone else is thinking or feeling, even if you haven't thought about other plausible explanations.	"He thinks I'm stupid because I didn't know the answer." "She didn't look at me. She doesn't like me anymore."
Labeling	Assigns an overarching characteristic to someone based on one thought, feeling, or action, usually in a very negative way.	"She's such a loser." "I'm an idiot." "What a jerk." "He's stupid."

continued

Mental filter (selective abstraction)	Ignores the many positive aspects of a situation and focuses only on one or two negative aspects. This makes it hard to see the larger picture.	Your therapist praises all of your progress and urges you to keep working on breathing. You think, *I'll never get better.*
Magnification/ minimization	Emphasizes the negative parts of something and downplays the positive parts.	"I'm a bad mother. I yell at my kids at least once a week." "My kids are doing well in school. They must get it from their dad."

When you realize you've gotten stuck in one of these distortions or styles, congratulations! It means you're paying close attention to your thoughts and learning to short-circuit the process of making yourself miserable.

When people begin practicing flexible thinking skills, sometimes they can get stuck in a secondary loop of negativity: *Wait a minute, that's not true! I don't have any evidence for that at all. I've gotten myself caught in more stinkin' thinkin'. Damn! Will I ever learn? No wonder my life sucks. I wish I weren't such a stupid loser.* Here negative thoughts start to hijack the positive process of flexible thinking itself. But careful attention can return those thoughts to reality: *Oops, that's just more stinkin' thinkin'. The truth is that I am learning, or I wouldn't be catching myself. Okay, good. Now, I know that I don't have any evidence for my negative thought. So let me look at what the evidence and my experience actually do tell me.*

Practicing Flexible Thinking

The process of flexible thinking has five brief parts. To make it easier to remember, the letters A, B, C, D, and E each begin one of the five parts of flexible thinking. While you're learning the process, it's a good idea to use a pen or pencil and paper to work through the parts. With practice, however, you'll eventually be able to do the ABCDE method in your head.

A: Activating situation. Write down the situation you're upset about.

C: Consequence. We skipped to this letter because most people can more easily identify the consequence of a negative feeling or behavior before they can identify the belief (discussed in the next step) that may trigger the negative feeling. Consequences can be feelings, but they can also be behaviors. Write down the most upsetting emotion (or behavior) that you feel. Words that express specific painful emotions include *fear* (or *terror*), *anxiety, sadness* (or *depression*), *despair, grief, loneliness, anger* (or *rage*), *revulsion* (or *disgust*), *dread,* and *confusion* (or *bewilderment*). Avoid words such as *neglected* or *offended* or *betrayed* or *disappointed* or *resentful,* which tell stories rather than express raw emotions. Look for the emotion *inside* one of these words, and write that down. (For example, the emotion inside resentment is usually anger; the emotion inside feeling neglected is usually loneliness.)

If you skipped over the feeling consequence and instead jumped to the behavior, then write that down. In reality, if we use a slow-motion analysis, we never skip the feeling. But some of us do seem to go right from the activating situation (A) to the action or behavior, especially those of us who have been told that we often act before thinking.

B: Belief. Ask yourself, *What belief or thought is triggered by this activating situation or event?* Now, write down this belief or thought and examine it; if it's a cognitive distortion, name it. If you have more than one thought, write down the one that most relates to the situation. To name it, feel free to consult the list of common distortions in figure 8.3 (page 96).

D: Dispute. Dispute or challenge that belief or thought by asking yourself, *What evidence do I have that this belief is accurate or this thought is correct? What evidence do I have that doesn't support this thought? What other ways are there to look at or explain the situation?* Write down your answers to these questions.

E: Entirely new thought or behavior. Ask yourself again, referring to figure 8.3 (page 96), *Are any cognitive distortions involved? Overall, does the evidence support my original thought or not?* If the answer is no, then replace that thought with one that *is* supported by the evidence. If the answer is yes, then you can have confidence in your original thought. Once in a while, of course, the evidence *will* support a painful or negative thought. Painful things do sometimes happen to everyone.

Another way to approach this part of flexible thinking is to ask yourself, *How hard would it be to convince a stranger that my original thought is true?* The harder it will be, the less likely the thought is true.

Once you've evaluated the evidence and replaced your original thought with a more accurate one (or realized that your original thought is probably correct), you need to decide what to do about it. Do you need to talk with someone about the situation? Ask someone for help? Change your plans? Change something about yourself? Get more information? Essentially, you're creating an action plan. Keep it simple, though—from a few words to a paragraph.

Brandon's Flexible Thinking

Let's walk through the flexible thinking process using Brandon and his neighbor (from page 93) as an example. Imagine that Brandon *didn't* turn around and see her grab the straying child.

A: Activating situation. Write down the situation you're upset about. Brandon writes, *My neighbor didn't smile or say hello or acknowledge me after I waved to her.*

C: Consequence: Write down your most upsetting feeling or behavior. Brandon writes, *Anger.* (No behavior, yet!)

B: Belief. Ask yourself, *What belief or thought do I have?* Write down this thought and examine it; if it's a cognitive distortion, name it. Brandon writes, *She never recognizes me. She's never friendly!* Then he examines this thought and realizes that he has overgeneralized. He writes, *Overgeneralization.*

D: Dispute. Challenge and dispute that belief by asking yourself, *What evidence do I have that this belief is correct? What evidence do I have that doesn't support this belief? What other ways are there to look at or explain the situation?* For things that support his thoughts, Brandon writes, *She didn't smile or wave or even make eye contact. She hurried past me as if I wasn't there.* For things that don't support his thoughts, Brandon writes, *She's always been pleasant to me before, and we've known each other for months. Just yesterday, she honked and waved when she drove past the outdoor café where I was having coffee.* For other ways to look at or explain the situation, Brandon writes, *Maybe she was preoccupied or lost in thought. Maybe she was upset about something that had nothing to do with me.*

E: Entirely new thought or behavior. Ask yourself, *Overall, does the evidence support my original belief or not?* Brandon writes, *No. I have no reason to think she'd snub me. She probably didn't see me. It seemed like her attention was focused somewhere else. And I thought it was all about me!*

Brandon concluded an entirely new thought and behavior was called for. He writes, *Next time I see her, I'll ask her what happened.* This is a perfectly good plan—but he thinks for a minute, crosses out that sentence, and writes instead, *I'll give her a call later and make sure she's okay.* That's a good plan, too.

Your Flexible Thinking

Now it's time to try your own hand at flexible thinking. Figure 8.4 (page 102) and worksheet 8.1 (page 103) summarize all five parts (ABCDE) of the flexible thinking process. These tools will help you discover whether your thinking about a particular situation is distorted or accurate. If your thought is distorted, you'll replace it with a more accurate and positive thought. If your thought is accurate, you'll be able to have more confidence in it. In either case, you'll then make a plan and take concrete, positive action—and you'll feel better.

Make at least six photocopies of worksheet 8.1, and for now, carry two or three copies with you wherever you go. (Remember, a full-page version of this worksheet can be downloaded at the Hazelden co-occurring disorders Web site at www.cooccurring.org.) Over the next week, anytime you feel bad about a situation or event or person (including yourself), try some flexible thinking. As soon as you reasonably can, find a spot where you can be alone for fifteen to thirty minutes and fill in the worksheet. As mentioned, once you've learned to do the process in your head, you can stop using the worksheet.

Figure 8.4

A Guide to Flexible Thinking: The ABCDE of Emotions

A
Activating Situation
The event, situation, person, place, or thing that starts the process.

▼

B
Belief
The belief, thought, or interpretation about the activating situation.

▼

C
Consequence
The resulting feeling or behavior.

▼

D
Dispute
Were any cognitive distortions used? What evidence is there that the belief is accurate or not?

▼

E
Entirely New Thought or Behavior
Based on D, is there any reason for a different thought or behavior? What is the next step?

Worksheet 8.1

Flexible Thinking: The ABCDE of My Emotions

A
Activating Situation

What is the situation?

▼

B
Belief

What are my beliefs and thoughts?

▼

C
Consequence

Resulting feelings:

Resulting behaviors:

▼

D
Dispute

Cognitive distortions (check all that apply):

_____ tunnel vision	_____ all-or-nothing thinking
_____ "should" or "must" statements	_____ worst case scenario thinking
_____ personalization	_____ disqualifying or discounting the positive
_____ overgeneralization	_____ emotional reasoning
_____ mind reading	_____ labeling
_____ mental filter	_____ magnification/minimization

What evidence is there that the belief is accurate or not?

▼

E
Entirely New Thought or Behavior

New thought?

New behavior?

What should I do next?

Not Getting Stuck

The truth is that most of us—not just people with co-occurring disorders—fall into cognitive distortions now and then. And all of us have distressing feelings several times during a typical day: someone cuts us off in traffic; a friend arrives late; we get lost in an unfamiliar neighborhood; we learn bad news about a family member. Painful feelings are appropriate in painful situations. But it's all too easy to get stuck in painful feelings even when the situation doesn't warrant them. When you learn that your friend has broken her arm, it's appropriate to grieve for her. But if you're grieving unreasonably or worrying excessively because she went hang-gliding and *might* break her arm, that's stinking thinking.

During your first week of practicing flexible thinking, fill out worksheet 8.1 *at least once* during each day in which you have troublesome feelings. It's also fine to fill out more—up to several per day. During that week, also practice the mindful relaxation exercise (from earlier in this chapter) at least twice a day.

Once you've practiced both of these skills for seven days, pat yourself on the back. You've become familiar with the basics of CBT, and you're ready to use them to propel and support your recovery. And remember your ABCDEs!

CHAPTER 9

Bolstering the Positive Effects of CBT

What Is Self-Talk?

In addition to practicing mindful relaxation and flexible thinking, another CBT-related skill is focusing on our internal dialogue. In our heads, we talk to ourselves much of the time about what we observe, what it means to us, and how we might respond to it. If you could read someone's mind, you'd hear a nearly constant stream of comments and judgments and conclusions: our internal dialogue.

Sandra looks out her window late one afternoon and sees an elderly woman walking her dog. Sandra thinks, *That's a cute dog. It reminds me of Quincy. But why is the dog wearing a sweater? It's not that cold out. That woman needs to give her dog more lead on that leash. It's almost choking. She and her dog should go to obedience training. I wish people would learn to take better care of their animals.*

Actually, you *can* read someone's mind: your own. Try this experiment and see for yourself: Sit comfortably in a quiet spot. Then, for the next five to ten minutes, just observe your thoughts. Don't try to do anything about them—just watch them without judging them, or hanging on to them, or pushing them away. Let them appear, swirl around, and then drift off.

You'll discover that your thoughts are a more-or-less continuous flow of comments, conclusions, and judgments about how the world is or should be. Let's call this internal patter *self-talk*.

Let's listen in on two different self-talk scenarios that might take place in Sandra's mind as she looks out her window and watches the woman and dog walk past:

1. *I wish people would learn to take better care of their animals. I'm glad Mom and Dad taught me to be a good pet owner. I'm probably a better mom because I had that opportunity. Which reminds me: Isaac and Leah should be getting home soon. I need to start cooking supper.*
2. *I wish people would learn to take better care of their animals. That poor dog. How can its owner be so thoughtless? I wish I had the courage to run outside and give that old lady a piece of my mind. But I know I won't. Confronting people is just too scary. Jeez, I'm such a wimp. It depresses me. I could use a drink.*

At the end of the first sequence of thoughts, Sandra feels confident, focused, and empowered. At the end of the second, she feels angry, ashamed, and a bit depressed. Yet both streams of self-talk started from the same observation (a woman walking her dog) and the same initial thought *(I wish people would learn to take better care of their animals).*

How can this be?

Although she's not aware of it, Sandra is most prone to negative thinking when she's hungry or tired. In the second scenario above, her stomach was empty and she was feeling sleepy. Without Sandra even realizing it, these physical stresses started a cascade of negative self-talk inside Sandra's head.

In chapter 8, we looked at how to spot, challenge, and replace our cognitive distortions. In this chapter, we'll build on that foundation. We'll look at strategies for spotting these distortions more quickly, for predicting when and where they'll appear, and for preventing them in the first place. The best process for doing all this is identifying your own unique patterns of negative thinking.

For example, Graham is most likely to fall into cognitive distortions when he's with his immediate family, especially when they're all sitting around the table drinking. Yelena has trouble thinking straight when she's with people she judges as more fashionable and successful than she. She starts to compare herself with them and feels inferior and ugly. Paulette dislikes her job, so she's more likely to slip into negative thinking when she's at work or around her boss.

To begin recognizing and changing your own patterns of negative thinking, practice flexible thinking for another week, doing exactly what you did before. This includes regularly filling in the flexible thinking worksheets (page 103)—at least one per day.

At the end of this second week, spend about an hour looking over these forms and seeing how and when you caught and challenged your cognitive distortions.

By now you've probably filled in about fourteen to fifty flexible thinking forms. Spread out all of these forms in front of you, so you can see them all.

Now sort the forms into groups. Look at the top of each form, where you listed the situation you were in. Look for situations that are similar, and make a pile of forms for each group of similar situations.

For example, maybe you filled in twenty-three forms. As you look them over, you realize that fifteen involved disagreements or arguments with your partner; eight took place late at night; and eight occurred when you were driving during rush hour. So you separate your forms into three piles: disagreements, night, and rush-hour driving. (Several forms overlap: late-night disagreements or disagreements in the car during rush hour. Each of these can go in whatever pile seems most appropriate.)

In this simple sorting exercise, you've actually done something profound and enormously helpful: *you've identified three types of situations where you are especially prone to cognitive distortions.*

When the sorting is done, use worksheet 9.1 on page 108 to create a summary or a single master form. Transfer the essential elements of each pile (situation) of forms onto the worksheet. These don't need to be detailed; just write a few words (or at most a few phrases) in each column. Start with the first group of situations and describe it in the first column (for example, "disagreements"). Then identify that situation's most common and frequent elements, in order to fill in the remaining columns (for example, "anger" might be your most frequent distressing feeling about disagreements).

You should be able to identify common themes or patterns now. What are the characteristics of the most common situations? Go-to beliefs? Favorite cognitive distortion? Best (worst) negative feeling? Jump-to behavior? When you slow the process down and examine it, what D and E steps pull you through and help you see things more flexibly?

Worksheet 9.1

My Most Distressing Situations and Feelings

Activating Situation	Underlying Belief(s) or Thought(s)	Distressing Feeling(s) or Behavior(s)	Cognitive Distortion	New Thought / Action Plan

When you've finished the form and this reflection, pat yourself on the back. You've done quite a bit of important self-investigation here. This master form serves as a reminder that you can replace your distorted thinking at any time, simply by acknowledging it, challenging it, and choosing to change it.

Post this form in a prominent place and review it regularly—at least once a week. In the weeks and months to come, it will help you to

- limit or avoid potentially painful situations
- notice when these situations do arise (or are likely to)
- navigate these situations more calmly and effectively
- feel less distress, less pain, more serenity, and more control

Managing Negative Emotions

Each of us is responsible for managing our own feelings, regardless of what they are or what causes them. In flexible thinking, we introduced the ABCDE method of managing negative emotion. CBT provides another highly effective process using the acronym STORC, which is specifically designed to help people manage their painful and distressing emotions. It also helps them possibly change their situations and behaviors. STORC was developed by William R. Miller and colleagues for the NIAAA COMBINE study.

The STORC model of CBT focuses more on our situations and behaviors than on flexible thinking. You can use both STORC and the ABCDE method, or you can try them and see which one works best for you. Both are excellent CBT skills.

The name *STORC* comes from the first letters of the process's five stages. These embody what happens in most human encounters and experiences:

S = Situation or event
T = Thoughts in response to that situation
O = Organic, all-natural feelings
R = Reactions
C = Consequences of our reactions

Let's look briefly at each of these stages.

S: Situation or Event

As you've seen, our feelings are not the result of events, but of how we think about, describe, or name those events. Through practicing flexible thinking, you've learned to change the way you feel about an event by changing the way you think about it.

However, there are two other effective ways to deal with events that can lead to distress or pain: (1) replace them with more desirable events and (2) balance out those events with other, more positive experiences.

You already have the skills to replace many undesirable events with more desirable ones. If you hate rush-hour driving, look for a better way to get to and from work. Take a bus, subway, train, or cab; carpool; walk; ride your bike or scooter; roller-skate; skateboard; or drive before or after rush hour.

Look back at worksheet 9.1 on page 108. Of the entries in the "Activating Situation" column, which ones can you replace with more desirable ones in the future? For each situation that you can reasonably change, create an action plan. Then follow that plan until you've replaced that unwanted situation with a better one.

Of course, not every undesirable situation can be replaced or transformed. But you *can* build plenty of positive experiences into your day. These can help you balance out your life, feel better, and avoid stinking thinking.

These pleasurable experiences are "psychological vitamins," because they strengthen us emotionally and provide us with added defenses against the storms and stresses of life.

A complete list of all the possible psychological vitamins would fill this book. Also, some activities that are strong vitamins for Cherise are annoying, boring, or even dangerous for Dudley. So everyone has to identify their own most potent psychological vitamins.

Worksheet 9.2 lists twelve common psychological vitamins. Underneath these, add a dozen other activities that can be powerful psychological vitamins for you.

Worksheet 9.2

Psychological Vitamins

Music
Exercise
Sports
Reading
Meditation or prayer
Nature
Movies and plays
Art
Hobbies
Time with friends
Time with caring family members
Time with pets

_____

_____

_____

_____

_____

_____

_____

_____

_____

_____

_____

Not every form of pleasure qualifies as a psychological vitamin. In fact, the following are *never* psychological vitamins: drugging, overeating, overspending, risky sex, compulsive behavior of any kind, and any form of pleasure with negative side effects or consequences. For most people with co-occurring disorders, drinking alcohol also can't be a psychological vitamin.

Like all vitamins, psychological vitamins are most beneficial when you take them daily. What's more, you may often need additional dosages:

- When times get tough, deliberately take extra psychological vitamins to help you feel better and maintain your recovery.
- When you sense that a difficult situation, event, or period will soon appear, build additional psychological vitamins into your schedule.
- If, as sometimes happens, a psychological vitamin turns toxic—you break your thumb playing golf, or the film that began so beautifully becomes dull and pointless—don't blame yourself for it. Deal with the immediate situation, and take a new, different vitamin when you can.

T: Thoughts

As we saw in chapter 8, often we'll feel an emotion before we're aware of the thought that created it. And sometimes that thought flashes in our minds so fast—and so automatically—that we take it for reality, rather than as something we made up.

You've already practiced identifying, challenging, and replacing your unrealistic negative thoughts. Now look for *patterns* of these cognitive distortions in your thinking. Becoming aware of these patterns will teach you a great deal about yourself—and will profoundly support your recovery.

Look again at worksheet 9.1 on page 108. This time focus on the second column, "Underlying Belief(s) or Thought(s)." Look at all the entries in this column. Are there any thoughts that appear over and over? If so, circle them. Then review these circled items and make a written list of the three to four most common underlying thoughts. Post this list near your worksheets.

In the future, when one of these thoughts appears in your mind, consider it an alarm bell. Stop and examine that thought carefully. Chances are good that it's stinking thinking.

Now look at the fourth column, "Cognitive Distortion." Scan all the entries in this column. Does a particular *form* of negative thinking—for example, overgeneralization, all-or-nothing thinking, or mental filter—appear multiple times? If so, circle each example. Do this for each type of cognitive distortion; then make and post a list of these most common types.

The two lists you just made will help you catch, identify, and correct cognitive distortions much more quickly in the future. Over time, with practice, you'll get to be an expert in identifying your stinking thinking and replacing it with thoughts that are more accurate, positive, and empowering.

O: Organic, All-Natural Feelings

Everyone has painful or disturbing feelings at times. But some people with co-occurring disorders have them frequently—and sometimes they can be quite strong. They may also involve physical arousal—sweating, a racing pulse, agitation, a sinking feeling in the stomach, and so on. These feelings can make people want to scream, or run away, or do something impulsive or foolish or violent. Even when people successfully resist these impulses, they may feel ashamed or guilty or embarrassed for having these feelings. Then they may feel ashamed for feeling ashamed.

The reality is that feelings are *never* evil or shameful or wrong. They're just feelings. All human emotions, even those that are disturbing or frightening, are completely natural and organic. Unless we *act* on them, they can't hurt anyone.

Suppose you're very hungry, so you stop in at a restaurant. The man at the next table is eating soup that looks and smells wonderful. Suddenly you feel empty and hollow and deprived. You have a strong impulse to grab the man's soup and eat it yourself. You don't, of course, but the truth is you'd like to.

Guess what? That impulse is completely normal. What's *not* normal is to follow it.

We all need to be careful about what we *do,* especially when it affects other people. But we shouldn't try to shut down what we feel. In fact, one of the biggest ways people can get into trouble is by trying to avoid or tamp down their emotions.

Take another look at worksheet 9.1. This time focus on the third column, "Distressing Feelings(s) or Behavior(s)." Look through the entries in this column, and circle any feelings or behaviors that appear over and over. Then write and post a list of those painful or distressing feelings or behaviors that are most common for you.

When one of these arises in the future, consider it a red flag. Stop and examine it, then look carefully at the thought behind it. Is it caused by a cognitive distortion? If so, restructure that distortion into a more realistic and positive thought. This will not only improve your thinking, it will also make you feel better.

R: Reactions

We can't always choose what we feel. But we *can* choose how we act in response to what we feel. A mindful response can keep us and others safe. A quick and mindless response can get us into big trouble.

When we feel strong anxiety, fear, despair, or another negative emotion, we're tempted to react automatically, without looking at our thoughts or considering the potential consequences of our actions. These automatic reactions fall into two categories: *aggression* and *avoidance*. Figure 9.1 shows the forms that aggression and avoidance typically take.

Figure 9.1
Forms of Aggression and Avoidance

Aggression	Avoidance
Arguing	Running away
Criticizing	Sulking
Blaming	Pretending not to care
Insulting	Becoming silent and/or passive
Picking a fight	Sleeping
Harming or destroying something	Eating
Physically hurting someone	Drinking
Deliberately creating problems	Getting high
	Participating in risky sex
	Impulsively ending or beginning a relationship
	Any compulsive activity (gambling, shopping, etc.)

Wanting to react in any of these automatic ways can be a valuable warning sign. Instead of reacting, *stop yourself before you speak or act.* Remove yourself from the situation, if possible. Then use your flexible thinking skills to

- look closely at what you're feeling
- identify the thought or thoughts behind it
- consider what kind of cognitive distortion each thought might be
- evaluate whether that thought is justified
- replace that thought, if necessary, with a more realistic and positive one
- create an action plan
- follow that plan

By following this process, you will respond with wisdom, caring, and compassion—both for yourself and for others. You will also feel better.

C: Consequences

It isn't hard to figure out what kind of consequences result from automatically reacting with aggression or avoidance. These negative consequences usually create more pain and distress, which in turn can lead to more aggression or avoidance, in a potential downward spiral.

By employing the essential skills of CBT, however, you can avoid this loop, act mindfully, and create more positive consequences. In the process, you will also deeply support and strengthen your recovery.

Applying CBT Skills to Everyday Life

The CBT skills introduced in this book—mindful relaxation, flexible thinking (the ABCDE method), and STORC—can be used daily to help you manage negative situations, thoughts, feelings, and behaviors. The more you practice these skills, the more automatic they become. Some negative reactions are like well-worn gullies. Whenever it rains, the water seems naturally to find the gully and rush through it. Changing the gully and the flow of the water can take some time. So might it be with some of your long-standing negative thought patterns. That being said, we have observed the rapid change of many long-held beliefs, which has resulted in amazing, positive transformations.

CHAPTER **10**

Exploring Twelve Step Peer Recovery

The Twelve Steps and Recovery

Recovering from co-occurring disorders isn't like healing from a cut or an ear infection. It requires ongoing self-monitoring, maintenance, and support. Although there are many good sources of such support—therapists, caring family members and friends, self-education, and so on—one of the best and most effective sources is mutual aid or peer support group meetings. Many of these groups advocate total abstinence; a few advocate harm reduction or moderation drinking. However, in this chapter, we will focus only on the Twelve Step peer recovery support group.

Twelve Step peer recovery support groups are not a formal treatment program, a religion, a code of ethics, or a form of therapy. They are simply a fellowship of men and women who refer to a set of guiding principles that support people's serenity, sanity, and recovery from any form of addiction.

This book devotes an entire chapter to Twelve Step groups because they work. Researchers have found, over and over, that people who attend Twelve Step groups do much better over time than people who don't. They are more likely to stay clean and sober; they have fewer symptoms; they need to be hospitalized or sent to rehab or detox less often; and, most of all, they seem to lead happier lives.

They also tend to live longer. Since Twelve Step groups began in the 1930s, they have saved many thousands—perhaps millions—of lives, and prevented untold damage to families and society. In fact, some observers say that, next to the polio vaccine, Twelve Step groups were the most important public health advance of the twentieth century.

Regular attendance at a Twelve Step meeting is a requirement of many formal treatment programs for co-occurring disorders. Other treatment programs strongly recommend attendance at Twelve Step meetings as a form of continuous care and recovery support. For some people, a few months (or years) of Twelve Step meetings are sufficient; however, others find the support and fellowship of these meetings so valuable that they continue to attend meetings for much of their lives. (Be sure to read "Twelve Step Groups and People with Co-occurring Disorders" on page 132.)

Twelve Step groups are forms of what therapists call *peer support groups, peer recovery groups,* or *peer recovery support groups.* Other such groups include Rational Recovery, Moderation Management, Women for Sobriety, and Secular Organizations for Sobriety. These four groups have not proven as effective as Twelve Step groups in helping people recover from their disorders and rebuild their lives.

Twelve Step groups are recommended for almost everyone because of their excellent track record. However, a different type of peer recovery support group is sometimes more helpful for those who attended Twelve Step meetings for several months but failed to benefit from them, and for those with a strong aversion to spirituality, a Higher Power, or God, no matter how those terms are defined. In any case, *some* form of peer recovery support group is an essential part of long-term recovery.

The success of Twelve Step groups, and the strong and consistent support that they offer, provides sufficient reason for their recommendation. However, there are other benefits to attending Twelve Step meetings:

- People realize that they're not alone, and that many others have the same situation or problems.
- People can speak without the fear of being silenced, dismissed, ignored, criticized, or shamed. Instead, they're heard, understood, accepted, empathized with, and surrounded by sanity and caring.
- Attendance at meetings helps people avoid withdrawal or isolation.
- Anonymity provides people with the safety, security, and freedom to say what is in their minds and hearts.
- Twelve Step groups enhance many people's social lives. They make friends at meetings; attend optional events such as picnics, barbecues, and conferences; and spend time with others in service or good-citizenship opportunities.

- When people are attending a Twelve Step meeting, they're not drinking or drugging. (This is one reason why many people who have powerful cravings for drugs or alcohol go to two or more meetings a day.)
- Twelve Step meetings offer practical tools, principles, and procedures for creating a better life.
- Meetings are free and available at a wide range of times and places.

All Twelve Step programs are based on three essential elements: fellowship (what therapists call *social support*), meetings, and "the program" (the Twelve Step approach to becoming and staying clean, sober, and serene).

Twelve Step Groups from A to Z

A Twelve Step meeting is a fellowship of people who have a desire to be free of addiction and help others stay addiction-free. There are no official leaders, no membership dues or fees, and no requirements for membership other than an interest in recovery. (People who are still using alcohol or drugs are welcome, provided they have a "desire" to recover from their substance use.) Meetings are supported by voluntary donations and run by volunteers on a rotating basis. Twelve Step groups are not allied with any sect, denomination, political party, or other organization or institution; they neither endorse nor oppose any causes.

The first Twelve Step group, Alcoholics Anonymous, began in the mid-1930s in Akron, Ohio, when a stockbroker and a doctor held the first known meeting. Since then, AA has grown to more than two million members. Today there are more than 100,000 AA meetings, and tens of thousands of other Twelve Step meetings, in more than 150 countries.

The best-known Twelve Step programs are Alcoholics Anonymous (AA) and Narcotics Anonymous (NA). In recent years, more specialized Twelve Step programs have appeared, such as Cocaine Anonymous (CA), Marijuana Anonymous (MA), Crystal Meth Anonymous (CMA), and Heroin Anonymous (HA). Other Twelve Step groups focus on addictions that don't involve drugs or alcohol. These include Overeaters Anonymous (OA), Gamblers Anonymous (GA), Shopaholics Anonymous (SA), Debtors Anonymous (DA), Sex Addicts Anonymous (SAA), and so on.

Still other Twelve Step groups serve the family and friends of people with addictions. The best known of these are Al-Anon (for adult family and friends of alcoholics), Alateen (for younger family and friends of alcoholics), Adult Children of Alcoholics (ACA or

ACoA; also known as Adult Children Anonymous), and Co-Dependents Anonymous (CoDA, for family and friends of people with addictions of any kind).

All of these groups are built on the same principles, and their meetings are similarly organized. Indeed, if a member of any Twelve Step meeting from anywhere in the world were to walk into any other Twelve Step meeting, regardless of its focus, they would find almost everything quite familiar.

There are now hundreds—and soon will be thousands—of Twelve Step meetings specifically for people with co-occurring disorders. These go by the names Dual Recovery Anonymous (DRA) and Double Trouble in Recovery (DTR), and there are others such as Emotions Anonymous, Dual Diagnosis Anonymous, and Schizophrenia Anonymous. DRA or DTR groups meet in almost every U.S. state, as well as in Australia, Canada, Iceland, India, New Zealand, and elsewhere.

Many Twelve Step meetings—called *open meetings*—welcome anyone and everyone. Other meetings—called *closed meetings*—are limited to people who wish to recover from the relevant addiction or problem. So, for example, if Nadia has schizophrenia and a crystal meth addiction, she is welcome at any closed meeting of Dual Recovery Anonymous, Double Trouble in Recovery, Crystal Meth Anonymous, Narcotics Anonymous, and Schizophrenia Anonymous—as well as at any open Twelve Step meeting.

Many Twelve Step meetings welcome both men and women, but some are solely for one gender. There are also some meetings for members of specific ethnic or cultural groups; for people who belong to particular religious denominations; and for people facing certain life situations (single parenthood, divorce, etc.).

A growing number of Twelve Step meetings are held over the Internet. While these can be supportive and inspiring, people with co-occurring disorders should try to attend in-person meetings whenever possible, since they offer a depth of personal contact, energy, and support that online meetings rarely provide.

Service and helping others are essential parts of every Twelve Step group. As a result, many people say that Twelve Step groups are some of the most inclusive and welcoming organizations on the planet.

Anonymity and Confidentiality

Part of what makes Twelve Step groups so effective is the anonymity of their members. People introduce themselves only by their first names, nicknames, or alternate first names they adopt. People can, of course, form friendships with other group members—

and reveal their full names to those members if they choose—but this is never expected or required. In the old days, when alcoholism involved intense social disgrace, anonymity was critical so members wouldn't lose their jobs. Today, society is more understanding, and now anonymity serves more to keep members humble and keep the emphasis on principles, not personalities.

Everything said in a Twelve Step meeting stays within the meeting. This provides the safety that allows people to say what is in their minds and hearts. In more than seventy years of Twelve Step meetings, many millions of people have reliably and honorably maintained this confidentiality.

Confidentiality also extends to not acknowledging to the outside world that someone is in the group. If Duane and Luciana are both in Dual Recovery Anonymous, and they both get in the same line at the grocery store, neither will acknowledge from where he or she knows the other. Although this may seem strange, it provides essential safety. Were they to start talking, an acquaintance might walk up and say, "Hi, Duane! I didn't know you shopped here. Who's this—someone from your Twelve Step group? Hey, wait—I know you! You work down the hall from me. So you're in Dual Recovery Anonymous, too?" (As explained in chapter 5, therapists keep their relationships with clients confidential in this same way.)

Twelve Steps, Twelve Traditions, and a Prayer

All Twelve Step programs share the same basic principles, known as the Twelve Steps and the Twelve Traditions.

The Twelve Steps describe the process of recovery; the Twelve Traditions protect each organization from itself, from individual ambitions, and from outside interests. Some say the Twelve Steps are like the fruit, and the Twelve Traditions are the like the shell that protects it. The Steps nourish and guide; the Traditions hold the group and organization together. Isn't it hard to believe that this organization survives and grows without any leaders, laws, or exclusions?

Figures 10.1 and 10.2 list the Alcoholics Anonymous versions of the Twelve Steps and Twelve Traditions. For other Twelve Step groups, replace "AA" with the group name; replace "alcohol" with "drugs," "cocaine," "meth," "gambling," "overeating," and so on; replace "alcoholics" with "addicts" or simply "others"; and make other such changes as appropriate.

Figure 10.1

The Twelve Steps of Alcoholics Anonymous*

1. We admitted we were powerless over alcohol—that our lives had become unmanageable.
2. Came to believe that a Power greater than ourselves could restore us to sanity.
3. Made a decision to turn our will and our lives over to the care of God *as we understood Him.*
4. Made a searching and fearless moral inventory of ourselves.
5. Admitted to God, to ourselves, and to another human being the exact nature of our wrongs.
6. Were entirely ready to have God remove all these defects of character.
7. Humbly asked Him to remove our shortcomings.
8. Made a list of all persons we had harmed, and became willing to make amends to them all.
9. Made direct amends to such people wherever possible, except when to do so would injure them or others.
10. Continued to take personal inventory and when we were wrong promptly admitted it.
11. Sought through prayer and meditation to improve our conscious contact with God *as we understood Him,* praying only for knowledge of His will for us and the power to carry that out.
12. Having had a spiritual awakening as the result of these steps, we tried to carry this message to alcoholics, and to practice these principles in all our affairs.

---

* The Twelve Steps of AA are reprinted with permission from *Alcoholics Anonymous,* 4th ed. (New York: Alcoholics Anonymous World Services, 2001), 59–60.

Figure 10.2

The Twelve Traditions of Alcoholics Anonymous*

1. Our common welfare should come first; personal recovery depends upon A.A. unity.

2. For our group purpose there is but one ultimate authority—a loving God as He may express Himself in our group conscience. Our leaders are but trusted servants; they do not govern.

3. The only requirement for A.A. membership is a desire to stop drinking.

4. Each group should be autonomous except in matters affecting other groups or A.A. as a whole.

5. Each group has but one primary purpose—to carry its message to the alcoholic who still suffers.

6. An A.A. group ought never endorse, finance, or lend the A.A. name to any related facility or outside enterprise, lest problems of money, property, and prestige divert us from our primary purpose.

7. Every A.A. group ought to be fully self-supporting, declining outside contributions.

8. Alcoholics Anonymous should remain forever nonprofessional, but our service centers may employ special workers.

9. A.A., as such, ought never be organized; but we may create service boards or committees directly responsible to those they serve.

10. Alcoholics Anonymous has no opinion on outside issues; hence the A.A. name ought never be drawn into public controversy.

11. Our public relations policy is based on attraction rather than promotion; we need always maintain personal anonymity at the level of press, radio, and films.

12. Anonymity is the spiritual foundation of all our traditions, ever reminding us to place principles before personalities.

---

* The Twelve Traditions of AA are reprinted with permission from *Twelve Steps and Twelve Traditions* (New York: Alcoholics Anonymous World Services, 1981), 129–87.

Twelve Step programs also share another essential brief text: the Serenity Prayer. This prayer, which is attributed to Protestant theologian Reinhold Niebuhr, is recited at every Twelve Step meeting:

> *God, grant me the serenity*
> *To accept the things I cannot change,*
> *The courage to change the things I can,*
> *And the wisdom to know the difference.*

Two books are widely read and consulted by people in Twelve Step programs: *Alcoholics Anonymous* (called "the Big Book" because it's nearly six hundred pages long) and *Twelve Steps and Twelve Traditions* (called "the Twelve and Twelve").

The Twelve Steps and a Higher Power

There's no getting around the spiritual nature of Twelve Step programs. They help people transform their lives through what the programs describe as a *spiritual awakening.* The Twelve Steps use the words *prayer, meditation, God,* and *a Power greater than our-selves* (which Twelve Step materials often shorten to *a Higher Power* or *my Higher Power*). And every Twelve Step meeting includes the Serenity Prayer.

Some Twelve Step writers who are less ecumenical use overtly Christian or Judeo-Christian terminology, and many Twelve Step meetings end with a Christian or Judeo-Christian prayer, such as the Our Father, and *amen.*

Yet many other Twelve Step meetings—including, for example, most Dual Recovery Anonymous meetings—largely avoid the word *God,* usually replacing it with *Higher Power.* Some meetings close with an ecumenical blessing and the word *peace.* And all Twelve Step meetings welcome people from all parts of the religious (and nonreligious) spectrum. In fact, many people who call themselves agnostics, atheists, skeptics, or un-believers have found Twelve Step programs to be enormously helpful.

The only basic spiritual tenet of Twelve Step programs is that each person acknowl-edges the existence of a Power greater than themselves, which they can define as they choose. Some individuals define their Higher Power as the Twelve Step program itself or the meeting they attend. Others have made the word *God* into an acronym meaning *good orderly direction* or (in AA) *group of drunks.* All of these are considered acceptable definitions of a Higher Power.

It is a testament to the power of Twelve Step groups that almost no one argues about any of this. When prayers are recited in meetings, skeptics and nonbelievers use alternative language, or stay silent, or simply say the words along with everyone else. During discussion periods in Twelve Step meetings, members often express doubts or questions about a Higher Power, and these comments are heard and understood with acceptance and compassion.

Nuts and Bolts of Twelve Step Meetings

Most Twelve Step groups meet weekly, though some meet as often as daily. Meetings usually last about an hour.

Leadership of meetings rotates among volunteers. The person leading a meeting is usually called a *chairperson* or *squad leader* or *trusted servant.*

There are several basic types of Twelve Step meetings:

- A *speaker/discussion meeting* begins with someone speaking about their experience, strength, and hope in recovery. This is followed by a discussion.
- In a *speaker-only meeting,* one or more prearranged speakers share their experience, strength, and hope. There is no formal discussion.
- A *discussion-only meeting* involves reading and discussing items from Twelve Step literature.
- A *Step meeting* begins with one person sharing their experience and understanding on a particular Step of the Twelve. Afterward, each member has a chance to speak about their own experience with that Step. Members focus on one Step per meeting until they've gone through all Twelve; then they begin again with Step 1.
- A *1/2/3 meeting* focuses on the first three Steps.
- An *orientation* or *welcome meeting* is for people new to the Twelve Steps or to that particular group or meeting.

At the beginning of each meeting, members are asked to introduce themselves. At some meetings, people simply say, "I'm Nadine," "I'm Tony," and so on; at other meetings, people introduce themselves by naming and admitting their disorders: "I'm Nadine, and I'm an alcoholic with PTSD"; "I'm Tony, a cocaine addict with bipolar disorder."

In Twelve Step meetings, *discussion* is *not* free-flowing or open-ended talk. Instead, members sit in a circle and, one at a time, speak of their own experience with addiction and recovery. While someone speaks, others listen attentively without interrupting, asking questions, offering advice, or adding their own thoughts. (These interjections are called *crosstalk,* and members are asked and expected to avoid it.)

No one is required to speak. A person can simply say "pass," which means "I have nothing I want to say today," at which point the next person in the circle gets to speak.

Anyone can attend any Twelve Step meeting just by showing up. Advance arrangements aren't necessary, and there's no maximum meeting size. (If lots of people show up, the only change is that some people don't get chairs.) Although many members attend the same meeting week after week, or day after day, this isn't required. Some people regularly shift from one meeting to another based on location, time of day, focus, and so on.

The Paradox of Powerlessness

Many newcomers to Twelve Step groups have trouble with Step 1: "We admitted we were powerless" over addiction, and as a result, life "had become unmanageable." To some people who first hear it, that sentence sounds like an admission of failure or a statement of futility. But it's neither.

Twelve Step programs stress that this powerlessness refers to an inability to recover *on one's own.* No one with a substance use or mental health disorder can simply will themselves better, no matter how hard they try. Multiple medical studies have confirmed this. Addiction is a brain disease, not one that can be wished or willed away. (In fact, one common symptom of the disease of addiction is a belief that the person can control their drinking or drug use on their own. This isn't just an error in thinking: *it may be a symptom of the disease itself.*)

Lasting recovery requires the help and support of other caring people—for example, one or more mental health professionals, other Twelve Step group members, and/or caring family and friends. For anyone in a Twelve Step program, recovery also requires the guidance of a Higher Power, however he or she chooses to define it.

When people give up trying to recover entirely on their own, they open themselves to other, greater healing forces—and to the love, caring, guidance, and support of others. Paradoxically, by admitting their powerlessness, they become empowered—able to access, accept, and apply these far greater powers.

Restoring Sanity

Some people with co-occurring disorders also have questions about Step 2 and the word *sanity*. On the surface, this Step would seem to say that the Twelve Steps, properly applied, can heal not only the chemical dependency but also the mental health problem. One might ask, for example, "Can a person with severe schizophrenia be cured of biological insanity, hallucinations, and delusions if he or she works the Twelve Steps?" The Twelve Steps are a recovery process, not a treatment plan. When people work the Twelve Steps properly, they do routinely recover from both parts of their co-occurring disorders. But working the Twelve Steps *includes* getting proper help and support from professionals and taking appropriate medication—*in addition to* attending meetings, enlisting the support of family and friends, and so on.

Furthermore, recovery from addiction—as Twelve Step programs define it—doesn't mean becoming free from all cravings, symptoms, or problems. Rather, successful recovery means staying clean and sober *in spite of* any cravings and problems and staying mentally healthy *in spite of* bouts with depression or anxiety. Similarly, recovery from a mental health disorder means that, with the proper help and support, a person can manage, limit, or cope with their symptoms—not that all those symptoms will disappear forever.

Sponsorship

Sponsorship is an optional, but deeply valuable, part of working the Twelve Steps. A sponsor is a more experienced person in recovery who provides one-to-one guidance on understanding and implementing the Twelve Steps. According to the pamphlet *Sponsorship* (Narcotics Anonymous World Services, Inc., 2004), "Sponsors share their experience, strength, and hope . . . A sponsor's role is not that of a legal adviser, a banker, a marriage counselor, or a social worker. Nor is a sponsor a therapist offering some sort of professional advice. A sponsor is simply another addict in recovery who is willing to share his or her journey through the Twelve Steps." Most people who attend Twelve Step meetings eventually get or serve as sponsors. Some do both at once.

Sponsorship is always voluntary, and there's no formal process for arranging it. Person A simply asks person B, "Will you be my sponsor?" and person B can agree or refuse, as they wish.

Sponsorship is a serious commitment for both people. They may study or discuss the Twelve Steps together or share their personal stories. Often the sponsor answers questions about the program. The sponsor's most important role, however, is being available to someone in a time of difficulty—when the person feels lost or overwhelmed; when they are strongly tempted to use alcohol or drugs; or, in DRA or DTR, when their mental health disorder seems about to become unmanageable.

Most sponsorships last for some time, typically months or years. However, short-term, temporary sponsorships are also common, especially for newcomers. If you have a dual diagnosis, an appropriate sponsor for you is one who understands your mental health disorder and supports your medical recovery as well as your spiritual one. Taking your medications will be as important to this sponsor as your attending meetings.

Getting Started with a Twelve Step Group

All Twelve Step meetings operate according to the same basic principles. However, each meeting has its own unique feel, and there are minor variations from meeting to meeting in how material is presented and meetings are run.

What's most important is that a Twelve Step meeting feel safe, sane, and welcoming. All other considerations are secondary to this.

By all means, people should comparison-shop by visiting several different meetings. This also helps them quickly get a feel for how the Twelve Step approach to recovery works.

Most meetings have a group process or someone in charge of welcoming newcomers and introducing them to Twelve Step programs. These people usually announce themselves near the beginning of each meeting.

One way to find a nearby Twelve Step meeting is to ask for a recommendation from a health or mental health professional, a treatment program or center, or First Call for Help (in most cities, 2-1-1 or 800-HELP555). Another is to google the name of the appropriate Twelve Step group (Narcotics Anonymous, Double Trouble in Recovery, etc.), plus the name of your city, state, or metropolitan area.

The following Web sites and national offices can also provide nearby meeting locations:

- Alcoholics Anonymous, www.aa.org, 212-870-3400, Box 459, New York, NY 10163
- Cocaine Anonymous, www.ca.org, 310-559-5833, 3740 Overland Ave., Suite C, Los Angeles, CA 90034
- Crystal Meth Anonymous, www.crystalmeth.org, 213-488-4455, 4470 W. Sunset Blvd., Suite 107, PMB 555, Los Angeles, CA 90027
- Double Trouble in Recovery, www.doubletroubleinrecovery.org, 718-373-2684, P.O. Box 245055, Brooklyn, NY 11224

- Dual Recovery Anonymous, www.draonline.org, 913-991-2703, P.O. Box 8107, Prairie Village, KS 66208
- Heroin Anonymous, www.heroin-anonymous.org, 5555 N. 7th St., #134-408, Phoenix, AZ 85014. HA does not have a phone number.
- Marijuana Anonymous, www.marijuana-anonymous.org, 800-766-6779, P.O. Box 2912, Van Nuys, CA 91404
- Narcotics Anonymous, www.na.org, 818-773-9999, P.O. Box 9999, Van Nuys, CA 91409

Alcoholics Anonymous and Narcotics Anonymous meetings are held almost everywhere in the United States and throughout much of the world. Other types of meetings are less widely available.

People with co-occurring disorders should definitely seek out Dual Recovery Anonymous and Double Trouble in Recovery meetings (where they are available and convenient), along with other Twelve Step meetings. Writer Timothy H. eloquently makes the case for this in an essay in *The Dual Disorders Recovery Book* (Hazelden, 1993):

> First, those of us who experience dual disorders are affected by social prejudice and by the stigma of mental illness. Prejudice and stigma are part of a larger social issue, but when negative attitudes and beliefs show up in a Twelve Step group, the results can be disastrous.
>
> Second, many men and women who have been diagnosed with a dual disorder say that they have received misguided advice about their diagnosis and the use of medication at Twelve Step meetings. Some have been told that they do not have an emotional or psychiatric illness, and that they are experiencing merely self-pity or some other character defect (*You don't need those pills; they'll cause you more problems* and *If you're taking pills, then you're in relapse and not really sober*). Individuals who have followed such advice have experienced relapse: some have been hospitalized; some have returned to alcohol or drug use; some have attempted or even completed suicide.
>
> Third, the existing Twelve Step programs [other than DRA and DTR] were not developed to address the problems of dual disorders. They offer neither direction nor guidance for dual recovery *based on the personal experience of others*.
>
> Fourth, existing Twelve Step groups [other than DRA and DTR] are unable to offer the degree of emotional acceptance and support that is needed and deserved for people in dual recovery.

Some individuals are fortunate. They have been able to find a Twelve Step meeting that has some appreciation of emotional or psychiatric illness, and they cherish the support they get for their sobriety. Nevertheless, they may feel uncomfortable sharing their *dual* recovery needs openly and honestly. They may still find themselves feeling the need for secrecy in a program of honesty. Unfortunately, they may gradually minimize, deny, and ignore the other half of their recovery needs.

Fifth, the existing programs are single-purpose organizations—one disease, one recovery. Dual recovery does not fall within their primary goals. People who have a dual illness recognize that it cannot be divided into simple and separate parts. They acknowledge that while they do find support for aspects of their illness from available groups, they also need a group in which they can look at their total illness and recovery needs.

Today the average person now understands much more about mental health disorders than they did fifteen-plus years ago—but these issues still do sometimes arise in Twelve Step groups other than DRA and DTR.

To newcomers, Twelve Step meetings sometimes seem a bit strange or clubby. But people in Twelve Step programs say that over time, as they attend meetings, the strangeness is replaced by a sense of familiarity, comfort, and sanity.

The Dark Side of Twelve Step Meetings

Thus far, this chapter has painted a rosy picture of Twelve Step meetings because, in general, they're models of compassion, fellowship, friendliness, and sanity.

But they aren't perfect, and neither are the people in them. Occasionally someone creates problems in a meeting and has to be corrected. It's also true that a very small percentage of meetings are themselves dysfunctional. Here are some warning signs that a Twelve Step meeting is not healthy—in which case you should find a different one:

- The same person is the meeting leader or key figure, month after month.
- People always give advice or act like therapists.
- There is regular crosstalk during discussion.
- People focus on topics other than their own experience with recovery and the Twelve Steps.

- There is a charge for attending. (Passing a basket for voluntary donations is fine, however.)

Making the Most of Meetings

Here are some ways to get the most out of Twelve Step meetings:

- Pick a meeting that's easy to get to, so you are more likely to show up even if the weather is terrible, or you're feeling depressed or exhausted.
- Figure out in advance exactly how you're going to get to and from any meeting, so transportation isn't an issue.
- Don't go to meetings only when you feel like it. Instead, establish a regular schedule—for example, every Wednesday evening or every weekday morning—and stick to it.
- Attend *at least* one meeting a week. If you feel strong cravings to use, or if your life is difficult or stressful, go more often. Lots of people attend a Twelve Step meeting every day—and those going through especially tough times go to two or three for a time. Twelve Step meetings have a cumulative effect: the more often you go, the more support they provide, and the deeper the Twelve Steps sink in.
- Attending meetings doesn't just mean showing up; it's important to pay attention and participate fully. This doesn't necessarily mean talking during discussion periods—but it does mean listening carefully to what others say.
- Most people say they get even more out of Twelve Step meetings when they also volunteer to serve. This can be as simple as setting up chairs or serving as a greeter—or it can be as complex as helping to plan or run a regional Twelve Step conference.
- The Twelve Steps rarely create big, sudden changes. Instead, people in Twelve Step groups find themselves changing slowly and steadily, one day at a time.
- In fact, "One day at a time" is a common Twelve Step reminder that recovery is a long-term process, not the sudden flipping of a switch. It's also a reminder that, when life seems overwhelming or hopeless, all we really need to do is take care of today—and, sometimes, just this moment.

Twelve Step Groups and People with Co-occurring Disorders

When Chris realized that he could no longer control his drinking, and his attempts at stopping on his own were totally unsuccessful, he decided he needed to try AA meetings. Chris, who worked in the restaurant business, knew many of his friends had gone to AA, sometimes because they got into trouble at work or while driving. Although Chris knew that not all of these people liked it and stayed sober, he did know of a couple whose lives really changed for the better. They were examples to him of how AA could work.

In addition to having a hard time accepting that he couldn't control his alcohol problem by himself, Chris really hated people. People annoyed him, and if he were completely honest, they frightened him. He felt that most people thought that they were better than him and were judging him negatively—for his clothes, for how he talked, for his appearance, maybe even for being a nervous guy. He worried people thought he was weird. These feelings went way back, and frankly, the alcohol helped him do social things like go to parties, ask girls out, tell jokes to his friends. It was liquid courage. So, in addition to dealing with the fact that he had lost control of his drinking, the only solution Chris knew about terrified him: peer recovery support *groups* like AA!

Fear of admitting a problem was discussed in an earlier chapter. Mixed feelings about the solution or treatment for a problem was also discussed. What about the common fears or barriers people with co-occurring disorders have to face in order to take advantage of peer recovery support groups such as AA or NA?

Indeed these fears inhibit many people with mental health problems from even attending one meeting, let alone going to meetings over time or being active participants. There are many people with co-occurring disorders who overcome these inhibitions—some on their own, some with the help of their treatment providers. These fortunate ones achieve the same benefits as anyone else: long-term sobriety, and feelings of being happy, joyous, and free.

What makes it so hard for people with co-occurring disorders to engage in peer recovery support groups? There are three main reasons:

1. Their symptoms make it hard to go to meetings.
2. The treatment they receive for mental health problems may be incorrectly perceived as counter to peer recovery support group philosophy.
3. Their mental health providers do not understand peer recovery support groups and therefore never recommend them.

Let's address each of these barriers, one at a time.

1. Their symptoms make it hard to go to meetings.

Negative emotions such as fear and anxiety, depression, guilt, shame, anger, and resentment are common among people with co-occurring disorders. In fact, these emotions form the basis of the defining symptoms of the disorders.

For example, fear and anxiety are associated with the anxiety disorders, such as generalized anxiety disorder, panic disorder, phobias, obsessive-compulsive disorder, and post-traumatic stress disorder. In addition, people with thought disorders such as schizophrenia or schizoaffective disorder suffer severe anxiety, particularly social fears.

Depression is the most common mental health disorder, and it is associated with pervasive negativity, isolation, and reduced capacity for initiative and energy. Depressed people don't expect good things to happen.

People suffering profound guilt and shame feel unworthy, as if they don't deserve any good in their lives. They may expect others to judge them harshly if "they only knew" what they were really like. They feel like impostors and stick to what's known rather than unknown in social situations. The less others know, the better. Shame and guilt are associated with mood disorders, such as depression and dysthymia, but they are also driving forces behind many social anxiety disorders, including social phobia.

Anger and resentment are among the biggest emotional or symptom barriers. Expecting disrespect, being quick to pick up on the negative, and having low-grade irritability—these symptoms make a person not at all tolerant of people in general. Remember the old saying from the angry man: "I don't have any problems with mankind. I just don't like people very much." People with this level of anger often have disorders such as bipolar disorder, or these symptoms are secondary to deep fear, frustration, or sadness.

If you have a mental health problem that includes these emotional symptoms, how do you deal with them to engage in peer recovery support groups? First, you must know that peer recovery support groups are out there for you. And they are very effective.

Second, you must know that everyone in peer recovery support groups has these negative emotions, to greater or lesser degrees—the same as you do. None of these feelings or symptoms is original. In fact, if something has a name, doesn't that mean it has been around for a while?

Third, you can try the motivational enhancement and CBT skills in this book. Use mindful relaxation before you head out to a meeting and use it when you sit down at a meeting, even if you need to sit by the door. Use flexible thinking to examine your cognitive distortions about attending a meeting. Are you engaging in "worst case scenario thinking" that prevents you from ever getting off the couch? Do you "personalize" and imagine that if you go to a meeting, the room will stop and everyone will turn around and stare at you as if you were a giraffe who just happened to wander in? You can also try the CBT process of STORC to focus on your avoidance behavior. Are they ways you can gradually approach a meeting? Go to the first meeting late and leave early. Go early and leave early. Go on time and stay, but sit close to the door and talk to no one. Go on time and stay and talk to the person next to you.

If you are in treatment, you should be able to ask your therapist how to make the connection. If your therapist doesn't know, you may need to talk with another therapist or counselor.

A therapist with expertise in co-occurring disorders will use some of the strategies outlined above but will also be able to direct you to meetings that may be a good fit for you. You may have felt more comfortable in certain types of taverns with certain types of people. Peer recovery support groups are like that. Maybe a women's meeting? A gay men's meeting? A small group meeting? A large, easy-to-get-lost-in kind of meeting? A meeting in a church basement or a meeting in a hospital cafeteria? A meeting in the neighborhood or a meeting forty-five minutes away where no one will know you? Whatever helps you to overcome the barrier of going is okay. Comfort will come in time. Avoidance doesn't help.

2. The treatment they receive for mental health problems may be incorrectly perceived as counter to peer recovery support group philosophy.

Did you know that Bill Wilson, one of the co-founders of Alcoholics Anonymous, suffered from depression and anxiety? Bill W. took psychotropic medication for these problems and did so up until his death. He died sober. Dr. Robert Smith—Dr. Bob, the other co-founder—also had bouts of severe depression. Surveys of AA membership, although less than entirely scientific but with thousands of respondents nonetheless, reveal that 50 percent of the members take medication for mental health issues.

Medications for depression, bipolar disorder, anxiety disorders, and most other mental health disorders are not addictive substances. Although some medications have some potential for addiction (called "addictive liability" or "addictive potential"), there are usually alternatives that are not addictive. If a nonaddictive alternative has been tried and proven ineffective, you can try a different alternative—as long as you are honest with your physician and take the medication as prescribed.

In an AA pamphlet, *The AA Member—Medications and Other Drugs,* there is excellent advice on this matter. The bottom line is this: no AA member should play doctor with anyone else's medication. If you are taking a medication that is prescribed for your mental health condition by a prescriber knowledgeable about your addiction history—and you have been honest with the prescriber—then you are doing what you are supposed to be doing. You are getting the best care for your co-occurring disorders.

In some Twelve Step recovery groups, medications for psychiatric or even addiction problems are frowned upon. People in these groups negatively judge the sobriety of others and deem it unacceptable or "less than" their own. This negative judgment and exclusionary attitude are inconsistent with the Twelve Traditions of AA and the primary purpose of the AA fellowship. If you happen to encounter these attitudes, continue to explore other peer recovery support groups in your community.

3. Their mental health providers do not understand peer recovery support groups and therefore never recommend them.

The therapist or program that has expertise in co-occurring disorders—that offers integrated, dual diagnosis enhanced, or even dual diagnosis capable services—will understand the value of peer recovery support groups and try as much as possible to help you make this connection. This therapist will appreciate that if you make this connection, you can enjoy continuous lifelong and free support while managing your co-occurring disorders. This therapist will also appreciate that the benefits of recovery exceed simple symptom control or relief, but rather involve the potential for a much larger and greater life transformation. This transformation has been described as spiritual, in that it encompasses all aspects of being in the world.

As we noted in an earlier chapter, unfortunately many therapists or mental health programs will be naive about the potential benefits of peer recovery support groups. These providers actually place your recovery at a disadvantage. Others like you who are in more integrated programs will be getting lots of guidance and support in making the peer recovery support group connection.

If you have co-occurring disorders and are in a traditional addiction treatment program, your provider will understand the value of peer recovery support groups—Twelve Step groups, in particular. But this same provider may not understand how your mental health or psychiatric disorder can affect your ability to find, attend, participate, or stick with these kinds of groups. This provider may grow impatient or even judgmental, considering your difficulties as demonstration of your lack of motivation, "resistance," or noncompliance. This lack of understanding can be every bit as problematic as the mental health provider who knows little to nothing about peer recovery support groups, or who even has contempt for such groups.

If you are in treatment and experience any of these barriers with your providers, talk openly about your experience and your concerns. Find a provider who can facilitate this connection, which will serve your recovery well in the short and long term.

Chapter 11

Getting Support from Family Members

What Do We Mean by "Family"?

The word *family* usually refers to people you're related to by blood or marriage. Therapists and treatment professionals, however, speak of families in two different ways. They use the term *family of origin* to refer to the family you grew up in, and *your current family* (or simply *your family*) to refer to the family household you're part of now.

This chapter defines family slightly differently, as *all the people who have a close, caring relationship with you,* whether or not they are related by blood or marriage. *Family* includes the people who live with you: your spouse or partner, your kids, your parents, your roommates, your grandparents, your grandkids, your elderly father-in-law, and so on. *Family* also includes people who *don't* live with you, but who are quite close to you: your boyfriend or girlfriend; your closest friends; your aging parents; your grown-up kids; your siblings; your grandparents and/or grandkids; your closest aunts, uncles, and cousins; your closest in-laws; and so on. All of these people are grouped together because they can be some of your biggest allies in recovery.

This is not an attempt to redefine the family unit. The word *family* is simply being used as shorthand. It's like saying *car dealer* for a company that sells not just cars, but trucks, vans, jeeps, and SUVs.

Someone doesn't have to have frequent contact with you to be considered family, according to this definition. In fact, if some close relatives and friends have pulled away because of your co-occurring disorders, include them as family members as you read this chapter.

Co-occurring Disorders Are Family Problems

When someone has co-occurring disorders, it usually affects everyone in the family. It adds stress to other family members' lives, makes family relationships more difficult, and shifts a variety of family dynamics.

Every family is a small social system. When something changes in such a system, other elements of the system shift as well to accommodate it.

When someone develops co-occurring disorders, family members often adjust by changing their roles, in an attempt to maintain a safe and stable environment. Some may become very involved in addressing the needs of the person with the disorders; others may withdraw and become less involved; still others may try to fix the person's disorders; and some may try to convince everyone that the person doesn't have any disorders at all.

When family members first learned about your co-occurring disorders, they likely felt all kinds of emotions: shock, anger, anxiety, dismay, fear, sadness, guilt, frustration, and so on. These may have mirrored the emotions you felt when you first learned that you have co-occurring disorders.

Because you are part of a family system, your family can do a great deal to support your treatment, recovery, sanity, and sobriety. In fact, multiple studies have shown that families are in a unique position to help people recover from co-occurring disorders. Furthermore, when families do get positively involved, people generally experience stronger and quicker recoveries. (For this reason, the involvement of family members is an essential component of recovery.)

Each family has its own unique strengths. Family participation, under the guidance of wise treatment professionals, identifies these strengths and makes the most of them to support the family member's recovery.

Surprisingly, family involvement wasn't widely encouraged until recently. Throughout most of the twentieth century, when someone was treated for either a mental health disorder or a substance use disorder, their family typically had little or no involvement. Many people's recoveries faltered, took longer, or failed because of this lack of involvement.

Enlisting Family Support

While there is no bad time for a family member to begin supporting your recovery, the sooner you can get family members involved, the better.

In general, feel free to directly ask family members for their support and involvement. In some cases, though—for instance, if someone is initially reluctant to help—it may be more effective for your therapist or another treatment professional to contact them and ask for their support. Because the request comes from a professional, it will feel more important and be harder for the family member to say no. In addition, if the family member has questions or concerns, the professional can address them on the spot—and help the family member feel more comfortable.

Gratefully accept whatever sane support family members give you, but do *not* chase after people or try to talk them into helping. (You can, however, tell people who decline to help that they are always welcome to add their support later on.)

Including family members in your recovery also helps to educate them about co-occurring disorders and helps to correct their misconceptions about these disorders. Here are the most common ways people misunderstand co-occurring disorders:

- They believe your disorders are a sign of moral weakness or laziness.
- They believe mental health disorders, substance use disorders, or both aren't real.
- They believe one part of your co-occurring disorders is the "core" disorder—and that when you recover from it, the other part will go away.
- They think you just have two separate, simultaneous disorders, like pinkeye and strep throat. They don't understand how the two parts of your disorder interact with and worsen each other.
- They don't understand that you're highly sensitive to very small amounts of certain substances (alcohol, marijuana, etc.). As a result, they may use one of these substances around you, or even encourage you to use it.
- They misunderstand the nature and effects of medications for co-occurring disorders. For example, they may believe that all such medications are addictive, or that you can't be clean and sober while you're taking any prescription drugs.
- They misunderstand the nature of treatment. For example, they may think that it focuses on dredging up past hurts or negative feelings, rather than on creating sanity, health, and a positive future.

The more information—and the fewer misconceptions—family members have, the more support they can provide. If family members have questions or want to know more about any aspect of your disorders, encourage them to call your therapist or treatment professional—or ask the professional to call them. If you like, also show them this book.

Family and the Causes of Co-occurring Disorders

When some of your family members—especially your parents—learn that you have co-occurring disorders, they may think, *Did I cause this problem or contribute to it? What did I do wrong?*

In most cases, the answer is "You didn't cause the disorder. You weren't a perfect parent (or sibling, grandparent, etc.), because nobody is, but you didn't give the disorder to me." In other words, your relatives can relax.

You'll recall from chapter 1 that some people have a genetic predisposition for mental health disorders, substance use disorders, or both. For example, someone selected at random has a 1 percent chance of contracting bipolar disorder over their lifetime. But if a parent or sibling has (or used to have) the disorder, there's a greater chance—a 10 percent chance—that they'll get it.

The same general principle applies for substance use problems. Because Jeremy has an alcoholic sibling, there's about a one in three chance that he'll become an alcoholic, too. If he didn't have an alcoholic sibling, his risk would drop to about one in fifteen.

Researchers know these predispositions are genetic because these percentages hold true regardless of the environments in which people are raised. For example, Jeremy's brother Nathaniel is an alcoholic—but the two have never met because Jeremy was adopted soon after he was born. Even though Jeremy's adoptive family has no history of alcoholism, and even though they taught him healthy attitudes about alcohol, Jeremy *still* has a one in three chance of becoming an alcoholic.

So it's possible that your biological parents gave you genes that made you more likely than most people to develop co-occurring disorders. But they're surely not to blame for it.

What about your environment?

If you've suffered serious trauma, such as physical or sexual abuse, then this may have contributed to your disorders, especially if the abuse occurred multiple times. Similarly, if you grew up in a seriously dysfunctional or high-stress household, that may also have predisposed you to contracting co-occurring disorders. But there's no clear, cause-and-effect relationship, because many people experience abuse, dysfunction, or stress without developing either mental health disorders or substance abuse disorders.

You and your family may find it helpful to create a family tree that goes back as far as your grandparents or great-grandparents and extends out as far as cousins, aunts, uncles, nieces, and nephews. On this tree, identify everyone who has (or had) a substance use disorder, a mental health disorder, or co-occurring disorders. You and your family may find this exercise surprisingly revealing—and enlightening.

How Family Members Can Help You Recover

The people you're closest to are in a unique position to powerfully support your recovery. Because they know you better than anyone else, they can offer insights, guidance, and assistance that no one else can. They may be the first people to notice if and when you are in danger of relapse. They can raise important questions and concerns. They can hold you accountable for supporting your own recovery. And they can hold your feet to the fire if and when you start to slack off.

Here are some of the many other things family members can do to support your recovery:

- Monitor your progress and tell you what they see—especially if you're not able to see it on your own.
- Let you know when you are in danger and may need help.
- Help you deal with cravings or persistent symptoms.
- Encourage you to stick to your recovery plan.
- Help you keep all treatment and therapy appointments.
- Encourage and remind you to regularly attend Twelve Step (or other support group) meetings.
- Join you in Twelve Step or peer recovery support group meetings.
- Help you remember to take all your prescribed medications.
- Help you avoid exposure to others' alcohol and drug use.
- Encourage you to pursue work, school, and other personally important activities.
- Adjust the family schedule to support your work, school, treatment and therapy appointments, and regular participation in Twelve Step (or other support group) meetings.
- Help you set, work toward, and achieve goals.

- Provide practical support of all kinds—from a ride to the store to a place to live.
- Help you solve practical problems.
- Help you anticipate possible problems and develop strategies for handling them.
- Provide love, support, and encouragement when you encounter disappointment or failure.
- Show confidence in your ability to get better, improve your life, and create a future of purpose and serenity.
- Help you develop a social network of clean-and-sober people who will support your recovery.
- Help you process stressful experiences by listening to you and talking with you.
- Ask, encourage, and expect you to make important contributions to the family.
- Have fun together in activities that support your sobriety and sanity.
- Help you find and participate in other fun activities that support your recovery.
- Recognize—and remind you—that setbacks are normal parts of recovery, and that personal growth can continue in spite of them.
- Recognize—and remind you—that you are capable of living a worthwhile, rewarding life.
- Educate other family members about co-occurring disorders and their treatment.

Above all, family members play an invaluable role in helping you have hope and in reminding you that positive change is *always* possible. This hope can be powerful spiritual nourishment that fuels your efforts and your determination to recover.

But family collaboration doesn't just benefit you; it benefits everyone involved. By working together, all of you

- strengthen your connections and trust
- feel more empowered and capable
- reduce family stress and friction
- treat each other with greater love, concern, and respect
- improve your communication skills
- improve your problem-solving skills
- help each other set and pursue goals
- recognize and appreciate each other's strengths and abilities
- have more fun together
- have more hope for the future

This section began by explaining that family members are in a unique position to assist you in your recovery. But you are also in a unique position to assist them. You can help them to help you by

- answering their questions about co-occurring disorders—or, when you don't know an answer, putting them in touch with someone who does
- letting them know whenever your disorders are giving you trouble
- letting them know immediately if one of your medications isn't working properly
- letting them know immediately if you feel seriously tempted to drink or do drugs—or if you have already relapsed
- showing your appreciation for their love, caring, and support

Making Family Members Part of Your Treatment Team

Chapter 6 sang the praises of shared decision making and urged you to work collaboratively with mental health and addiction treatment professionals to create an ideal recovery plan.

Now let's revisit the concept of shared decision making—this time with family members.

Most people in treatment for co-occurring disorders have a "treatment team" that includes a therapist, one or more other professionals, and/or at least one peer recovery support group. Think of your family as members of your treatment team as well:

- Give family members and professionals each other's contact information (with their prior permission) so they can communicate and work together effectively.
- Bring family members into therapy and/or treatment sessions.
- Bring family members to Twelve Step and/or other peer recovery support group meetings.
- Give family members copies of your treatment plan—and, perhaps, involve them in creating or modifying that plan.

Creating Relapse Prevention and Response Plans
with Family Members

In general, people with co-occurring disorders have a higher risk for relapse than people who have only a mental health disorder or only a substance use disorder. In part, this is simple arithmetic: two disorders create more problems and risks than one. But a relapse of one part of the disorder can sometimes trigger a relapse of the other. If Javier goes back to smoking marijuana, that can trigger his panic disorder. If Barbra's PTSD symptoms reappear, she may start drinking again to numb the pain and fear.

That's the bad news. But there's good news here, too. People with co-occurring disorders who receive integrated treatment tend to relapse less often, less severely, and for shorter periods than those who don't receive such treatment.

And here's better news still. Extensive research has shown that family support prevents or reduces the number of relapses of both parts of co-occurring disorders. It also prevents or reduces hospitalizations, detoxes, and other negative events.

Nevertheless, a relapse is always possible at any point in recovery, just as it's always possible to re-injure a broken arm, even years after it has healed. For this reason, it's essential to make three simple plans:

1. A day-to-day self-care plan that will help you *avoid* relapse and stay sober, clean, sane, and healthy. Chapter 13 will guide you through the process of creating this plan.
2. A plan to help you *prevent* a relapse when warning signs of a potential relapse appear.
3. A plan to *respond* to a relapse if one occurs.

You'll need to work collaboratively with family members and treatment professionals to put together each of these plans. Partly it's because family members can provide helpful guidance and ideas; partly it's because their actions and decisions will be part of each plan.

Relapses tend to follow patterns. By understanding your particular pattern, you and your family can create plans that are as helpful and effective as possible. (Of course, any of these plans may change over time, as your recovery proceeds and everyone involved gains experience.)

Relapse Prevention Plan

A relapse prevention plan will help you and your family

- identify situations that can trigger a relapse of either part of your disorder
- create strategies to avoid or cope with those situations

- identify warning signs of potential relapse for both parts of your disorder
- devise specific steps to keep you safe after a warning sign appears

While the relapse of a mental health disorder can happen spontaneously, it's much more likely to be triggered by a stressful activity or situation. Triggers differ from person to person, but some common ones include extended family gatherings, large crowds, loud and prolonged noise, excessive heat, getting caught in rush-hour traffic, getting lost, being reprimanded at work, or having a fight with someone close to you.

A stressful activity or situation can also trigger a substance use relapse—but so can simple exposure to drugs, alcohol, or people who use or sell them. Most nightclubs and bars, and many parties and restaurants, can trigger a substance use relapse in some people. In fact, for some people recovering from a drug addiction, simply driving through a dealer's neighborhood, or having enough cash on hand to buy drugs, can be a trigger.

Talk honestly with your family members about the people, places, and situations that may trigger you. Also ask them for their observations about what has triggered you in the past—and listen carefully to what they say.

You and your family should also discuss the warning signs each of you has observed that indicate that a relapse may be imminent. Some of these will be *internal* signs— thoughts, impulses, emotions, and sensations—that only you experience. Others will be *external* signs—things you say, do, or stop doing—that people close to you may notice before you do.

Many families create a written checklist of these early warning signs, with each member keeping a copy, referring to it when necessary, and adding to it as appropriate.

Although avoiding triggering situations and people is ultimately your responsibility, there are lots of things your family can do to help. For example, they can make their homes drug- and alcohol-free when you're present. When you and your siblings are invited to a family wedding—which you know will be followed by a noisy, boozy reception—you and your sister can agree in advance to attend the wedding ceremony, skip the reception, and go out for pizza instead. Your brother can accompany you to your office holiday party to ensure that you don't accept any alcohol. Your grandson can turn down his music or use his iPod when you visit. Sit down with your family and, together, create a list of practical things each member can do to help prevent you from relapsing.

You and family members also need to discuss and agree on what each of you will do if and when signs of a potential relapse appear. Here are some things to discuss and agree on:

- whom you'll contact, and how you'll contact him or her
- who your backup contact will be if that person isn't available
- whom you'll call in an emergency—that is, if the symptoms of your mental health disorder seem about to take over, or if you are on the verge of drinking or taking drugs
- whether there should be a point person who takes charge of helping you stave off a relapse—and, if so, who that person should be
- at what point family members will contact your therapist or other treatment professional for guidance
- who will take charge of informing other family members about the situation

Write these agreements down and distribute them to everyone on your treatment team, including family members, all treatment professionals, and your Twelve Step sponsor, if you have one. This document should also include contact information for everyone on the treatment team, so people can easily contact each other in an emergency.

Everyone on your treatment team needs to be able to respond quickly and nimbly if a sudden, serious relapse occurs. While warning signs of a mental health relapse typically appear several days in advance, this isn't always the case—and a substance use relapse can occur spontaneously.

Relapse Response Plan

This plan focuses on responding quickly and effectively if a relapse occurs. You and your family should consider and discuss the following:

- whom you will contact, and how you will you contact him or her (this may be a family member, your therapist, some other treatment professional, or your Twelve Step sponsor)
- whom you will contact as a backup if that person isn't available
- who will take charge of making sure you stay safe and get the help you need
- at what point that person will call 9-1-1 or get you to a hospital
- who will take charge of informing other family members about the situation

Both your relapse prevention plan and your relapse response plan should include two clear and unequivocal commitments from you: (1) you won't harm yourself, no matter what thoughts, feelings, or impulses you experience, and (2) you'll call 9-1-1 in a potentially life-threatening situation.

Confidentiality

Involving family members in your recovery includes coming to a clear agreement about confidentiality.

It may not be in your best interest to tell everyone you know that you have co-occurring disorders. Should your employer know? Your co-workers? Your cousins in Philadelphia? Their fourteen-year-old daughter? Their five-year-old son? Your niece and nephew in Caracas? Your neighbors? Your minister? Your guitar teacher, whom you meet with privately? The teacher of your karate class? The other students in the class? Elderly Uncle Bob, who is beginning to show signs of dementia? His wife, Aunt Shirley, who is as sharp as a tack, but also a worrywart and a gossip?

And of those people you do tell about your disorders, how confidential should you ask *them* to keep that information? What can your less-than-close relatives tell other relatives? What can they tell their partners? Their kids?

There's no one-size-fits-all answer to these questions, of course. You'll need to decide, on a case-by-case basis, whom you'll tell, what you'll tell them, and how confidential you'd like them to keep that information. Some people will need a detailed explanation of each part of your disorders; others may just need a few sentences. Some people can be informed about your mental health disorder but not about your substance use disorder, or vice versa. And children, of course, need explanations that are appropriate for their level of understanding.

The best way to handle this is to discuss it frankly, openly, and in detail with family members. Here are some things to consider:

- Make decisions based on whether they will support your recovery—not on whether they will save face or avoid embarrassment.
- You don't get to simply give orders. Deciding whom to tell and what to tell them should be a subject for discussion and negotiation. Make your preferences known, but remember that you can't force anyone to do anything. At times you may need to say something like "I'd really prefer that Carolyne not know about this, but it's up to you."
- Clarity is essential. Clearly review and restate each decision once it has been

made. For example, "Okay, so we'll let the relatives in Montreal know, except for the ones in nursing homes." It's also a good idea to create a final list and distribute it among your treatment team, so people have something written to consult.

- Don't assume that anyone knows—or can intuit—which people to tell and which ones not to. It may be obvious to you that Aunt Shirley shouldn't be told—but unless you say explicitly, "Please don't tell Shirley," someone very likely *will* tell her.

- Ultimately, you can't control what other people say or do. Freida may choose to tell Alissa, even though you asked her not to. Pete may tell Sue, but forget to ask her to keep the information confidential. Be clear about what you want, and then let go of the outcome.

When Involving Family Members Feels Risky

There may be some people you're close to whose support you *don't* want to ask for. Maybe you're concerned that certain people will shame, blame, or lecture you—or even deny that you have a mental health problem or a substance use problem. Perhaps someone in your family has poor personal boundaries and is likely to get *too* involved, enmeshing and confusing his or her life with yours. Or maybe you just have an intuition that someone will do you more harm than good.

Safety is an essential element of recovery. If there's someone you don't feel safe with, *don't* ask for their help. Treatment professionals will support you in this. In treatment sessions, they'll also create and enforce ground rules that won't allow shame, blame, negative judgment, enmeshment, and so on.

You also get to set clear, specific limits for any family member's involvement. For example, if you want your brother's and parents' support, but only want your brother to join you in treatment sessions, just say so.

Of course, family members get to set their own limits, too. Maybe you'd like your two best friends and your three siblings to join you in treatment sessions, but only one friend and your two sisters say yes. That's their privilege.

Aside from safety concerns, there are four common reasons why you might feel reluctant to involve a family member in your recovery:

1. *The person was once close to you, but has withdrawn because of your co-occurring disorders.* Try to reconnect with this person. Begin by letting them know that you're in treatment or recovery, then ask for their support. Once they hear that

you're working to get better, they may be happy to help. The worst they'll do is say no, or fail to respond.

2. *The person has a mental health disorder, substance use disorder, or co-occurring disorders of their own, which may or may not have been diagnosed.* If they're in denial or have no interest in their own recovery, then it's usually best not to ask for their support. However, if they're also in treatment or recovery, their support can be very helpful, and your parallel journeys of recovery can help the two of you grow closer. If their own disorder has not yet been formally diagnosed but they think they may have a problem, asking for their support may be a good idea. Their support for you may encourage them to get their own condition assessed.

3. *Although you and a certain family member are close, you are also often in conflict.* Each such situation is unique, so discuss it with a treatment professional. However, having this family member join you in treatment or therapy sessions may reduce or heal some of your conflicts.

4. *You want to spare family members the stress of involvement.* This is stinking thinking. In fact, involvement is far more likely to give family members hope and relief. And remember: you're not forcing anyone to do anything. People can say no if they want to. And the participation and support of those who do say yes can improve your relationships and reduce blame, stress, and worry. Some family members may even recognize problems or issues of their own, for which they then may seek professional help.

The Dark Side of Family Involvement

Even loving people with good intentions can make mistakes that get in the way of your recovery. Here are the most common ones.

Enabling

Enabling is shorthand for *enabling someone to stay stuck in an addiction or mental health disorder, rather than encouraging their recovery.* If you're an alcoholic, someone who offers you a drink or invites you to a keg party is said to be enabling you; the person is called an *enabler.*

In practice, most enabling takes a much more subtle form: protecting someone from the natural consequences of their disorder.

For example, suppose you don't take your medications regularly because you feel fine. As a result, you lose track of time and miss your bus to work. So you ask your partner to drive you to work, and the person does.

If you do this once, it's no big deal. But if you continue not to take your medications and continue to miss your bus—and your partner continues to drive you to work—then this person is enabling you. As long as your partner continues to drive you, you have no incentive to take your medications regularly.

Strange as it may sound, the most loving thing your partner can do is stop driving you to work. You need to be late and get chewed out by your boss for it. You also need to learn that if you don't keep better track of time—that is, if you don't take your medications regularly—you could lose your job. Only when your partner *stops* enabling you will you learn that not taking your medications can have serious consequences.

Sometimes people enable others without even realizing it. They shop for their child who can easily shop for himself or herself. They make excuses for their partner or cover up for them. They say their mother is sick, when in fact she's strung out after a night of cocaine. Sometimes they'll even take the blame themselves: "Bart missed his therapy appointment again? It's my fault, really. I promised to wake him up at 7:00, and even though I did, I didn't check to make sure he was awake when I left the house at 7:20."

Family members naturally want to be loving, generous, and helpful. But "help" that keeps people stuck, sick, or addicted isn't actually helpful.

When family members first learn of your co-occurring disorders, they may have temporarily taken over some of your roles and responsibilities within the family or household. Some degree of protection is understandable, and even desirable. But if that protection allows you to continue drinking, drugging, or denying a mental health issue, it has gotten in the way of your recovery.

Discouraging Change

At first, co-occurring disorders can be frightening and bewildering for everyone in a family. Once you begin to recover and your disorders are under some control, family members usually feel enormously relieved.

However, sometimes people treasure this relief so much that they become overly invested in maintaining the status quo—and overly protective of the person with the disorders. They're afraid that any change could rock the boat and upset the precarious balance that has been achieved.

As a result, when you announce that you've decided to go back to school, or take a new and challenging job, or ask your girlfriend or boyfriend to marry you, some family members may try to discourage you. "Are you sure you're ready for that? You've only been in treatment for two months. It's too soon to make a major change. I worry about whether you can handle it."

This person *is* genuinely worried. They're concerned that the stress of taking this new, risky step will cause you to relapse, and that all your old problems—and all the stresses those problems created for family members—will come roaring back.

These fears are understandable—but they're not terribly justified. Risk, change, and new ventures are natural aspects of human growth. *They're also essential parts of recovery.* Your family needs to understand that you can and should keep growing as a human being even though you have co-occurring disorders.

Sometimes family members say something like this: "We want you to take risks and move forward in your life. But first we want you to be clean, sober, and free of mental health symptoms for a few months." While this is usually said out of love, it's misguided. Recovery almost never proceeds in perfect stages, in which the person first stops drinking or drugging; then their mental health symptoms disappear; then they get a new job; and so on. In real life, things tend to happen awkwardly, uncertainly, and nonlinearly. People take two steps forward and one back (and, sometimes, one forward and two back). This is the nature of recovery—and of life.

You don't have to have achieved sustained abstinence or the complete remission of mental health symptoms to pursue goals and move your life forward. Unless you're in the hospital, it's possible to begin taking those steps right now.

In fact, *not* setting goals and working toward them can seriously undermine your recovery by making you feel frustrated, demoralized, and purposeless. The more distant the attainment of a goal seems, the less motivating it becomes, and the less reasonable it seems to pursue it.

You may need to tell your family, "This is something I'd like to try. I might succeed and I might fail. Either way, I'll learn and grow from it. And if I do fail, it's not the end of the world. It's important for me, and for my recovery, to move forward in my life. I'd like your support."

Of course, if your proposed new venture is irrational, irresponsible, or impossible ("So what if I never finished high school? I know they'll let me into medical school when I show them all the reading and research I've done"), then that's your disorder talking, and your family is right to discourage you. They should also encourage you to promptly contact your therapist or psychiatrist.

Expecting Too Much—or Too Little

Family members may have some unrealistic expectations for your recovery. You may have some, too. Here are the most common ones.

Reading too much into small successes and failures. Getting excited over every small success—or gloomy over every failure or problem—only creates unnecessary stress. Recovery is a long-term investment: it's the overall trend that's most important, not the gains or losses of the current hour or day.

Believing too strongly in the power of intention. Wanting to get better, working at getting better, and receiving solid support are essential elements of recovery. Most of the time, these elements naturally lead to healing, sanity, and serenity—but not always. Sometimes, despite all our best efforts, things simply don't work out the way we want them to. As Twelve Step groups put it, "Shit happens"; the unexpected and unforeseen are parts of life. When things do go badly despite people's earnest efforts, it can be tempting to blame yourself, or each other: "If only I'd tried just a little bit harder." "I guess you didn't really want to recover, did you?" "After all the support we gave you, this is how you repay us?" "Your relapse couldn't have been just an accident." *These are all forms of stinking thinking.* They assume we can control the world, and the truth is that we can't. We can only do our best and take things one day (and sometimes one breath) at a time.

As Carlene DeRoo and Carolyn DeRoo write in *What's Right with Me* (New Harbinger, 2006),

> In this culture we are raised with the notion that if we do the right thing, things will work out for us. But some difficulties have nothing to do with us. We may be doing a whole lot right—even going above and beyond—but we're still struggling. When that happens, we feel bad about ourselves. We question if we did the right thing. We need to disconnect from the belief that we're doing something wrong just because this struggle exists. We need to bear in mind that this is just a basic part of life.

Treating relapse as an unlikely event—or a major failure. Most people in recovery from co-occurring disorders relapse at least once. On the one hand, neither you nor your family should expect a relapse or feel that one is inevitable; on the other hand, if one does occur, it's not the end of the world. Call your sponsor, get to a meeting, and visit your doctor if the relapse involves your medications. The longer you wait, the more guilt and shame you experience about your relapse, and the more difficult it will be for you to get back into recovery. So, shake the dirt off and get back on the horse. Frequent or long-term relapses are causes for serious concern, however.

Ignoring Their Own Needs

Sometimes family members can get so focused on supporting your recovery that they don't take care of themselves. They may also neglect other family members, some of their responsibilities, or some of their other relationships. Therapists call this *codependence.*

It's important for you to put recovery, sanity, and sobriety at the center of your life. But when other people put *your* recovery, sanity, and sobriety at the center of *their* lives, something is wrong. They've lost touch with their own needs and sacrificed themselves for you. This helps no one—not even you.

You can help family members help you by encouraging them to take care of themselves, pursue their own interests, live their own lives, and relax and have fun once in a while. Co-occurring disorders do not have to be a prison sentence or cause for martyrdom.

Family support is an essential part of recovery from any co-occurring disorders. But support can come from many other sources as well. In fact, people in successful long-term recovery often stress the importance of creating and relying on a personal support system or network. In the chapter that follows, we'll look at how to create your own ideal support network.

Chapter 12

Building a Personal Support Network

Recovery Is a Community Project

If you didn't get this already, we're going to tell you again that recovery is not a one-person job. While the most important ingredient of recovery is your own sincere desire to get better, you can't do it alone. *No one* can do it alone, no matter how strong, committed, or well intentioned they may be.

In previous chapters, we looked at how family, friends, support groups, therapists, other mental health professionals, and Twelve Step sponsors—and, of course, your Higher Power, however you define it—can all support your recovery. What we didn't discuss, though, is that in forging and strengthening these relationships, you create something much more powerful: your own personal support network. In the next few pages, we'll consider just how extensive—and how potentially helpful—your own unique support network is.

Turn to worksheets 12.1 and 12.2 on pages 157 and 159. Then find a quiet place where you can be alone for about half an hour. (Remember, you can always download full-page versions of the worksheets at www.cooccurring.org.)

Using worksheet 12.1, list all the people in your life who are willing and able to assist you in your recovery. Think of all the people you can trust; people whom you can ask for help when you are confused, upset, or in trouble; and people who will tell you the truth, even when it's painful. List doctors and therapists and sponsors. List your support groups and perhaps people you know and like in these groups.

Make several copies of this list. Post some in prominent places in your home; carry another copy with you. Look at this list whenever you feel alone, sad, or despairing. You may not be able to call anyone on the list at the time, but it will remind you that all these people are rooting for you and your recovery, and they will do their part to support it. And when you need someone's help, pick up the phone. All you need to do is reach out and ask.

Worksheet 12.1

People on the Side of My Recovery

Professionals   Family Members   Friends
(doctors, therapists, and
other people in the health
and mental health fields)

_____

_____

_____

_____

_____

_____

_____

_____

_____

_____

_____

Support Groups   Sponsor(s)   Others

_____

_____

_____

_____

_____

_____

_____

_____

The People in Your Way

Next do something harder, but equally helpful. On worksheet 12.2, list all the people you're in regular contact with who are *not* on the side of your recovery. This list might include people who hope you'll go back to drinking or drugging (and who might have drug or alcohol problems of their own); people who would like to see you drinking or using rather than sober or clean, sick rather than healthy; people who hope to exploit or manipulate you; people who are preoccupied with their own lives; and people who just plain don't care about you. There may also be people who trigger your PTSD-related memories and symptoms, tell you that you don't need your medication, or tell you that "those people" are polluting your mind. Are they on the side of your recovery?

Your list may include some relatives, neighbors, co-workers, and/or people you do business with. It might also include some people you call (or used to call) friends. In rare cases, it might even include your spouse or partner.

Like your first list, make copies, post them in prominent places at home, and carry a copy with you, so you can remind yourself that these are people who can hold you back and undermine your recovery.

Worksheet 12.2

People NOT on the Side of My Recovery

Family Members   Co-workers and People I Do Business With   Neighbors, Friends

_____

_____

_____

_____

_____

_____

_____

_____

_____

_____

_____

_____

_____

_____

_____

_____

_____

_____

_____

Now for the hard part. You'll need to decide what you'll do about your relationship with each person on this list. There's a crusty old line about such people in your life: "Shoot 'em, escape 'em, or divorce 'em." Although this old saying may be cynical, you actually have three basic choices: (1) do your best to *transform* the relationship; (2) *end* the relationship; or (3) *limit* the relationship. Transforming the relationship requires the efforts and good intentions of both you and the other person; ending or limiting the relationship requires only your initiative.

Transforming a relationship isn't easy, but when it's done successfully, it can create huge rewards: greater honesty, trust, empathy, intimacy, and support. On worksheet 12.2, *circle the names of people* with whom you feel you may be able to forge healthy, supportive, transformed relationships. (Sadly, few names will probably merit circles.)

The first step toward creating such a transformed relationship is having an honest discussion with the person in question. You might begin the discussion this way:

> You (already/may/may not) know that I have co-occurring disorders, which involve (name of mental health disorder) and (name of substance use disorder). I'm working hard to heal and recover from both parts of this disorder. This has meant changing my life in a lot of ways, including staying clean and sober, and redefining some of my relationships.
>
> I'd like us to remain (friends, tennis partners, friendly neighbors, etc.), but for that to happen, I need to ask you to do some things differently when we're together. I need people to support my recovery, not get in its way. This means (not offering me alcohol, not smoking marijuana in front of me, meeting for lunch in restaurants instead of bars, not calling me a psycho junkie when I beat you at tennis, etc.). If these are things you can do, great. I'll be grateful, and I'll look forward to more good times together. But if you feel you can't make these changes, I'd appreciate knowing that now.

Instead of delivering demands or ultimatums, this approach gives the other person a choice, with clear consequences that follow whatever choice they make.

If the person says they're willing to change, believe them (for now) and thank them—but remember that change rarely comes easily for anyone. Even the most well-intentioned people can sometimes forget things. You may need to remind this person—perhaps many times—about your disorders and the person's commitment to supporting your recovery:

- "Let's not sit in the bar; let's get a table in the restaurant instead. I know it's a ten-minute wait, but it will be much safer for me."
- "Remember, tell your brother that if he's going to drive us to the game, he can't be high. If he wants to toke up after he drops us off and goes home, that's his business. But I need him to be straight while we're together."
- "There won't be a big, noisy crowd at the reception, will there? If there's more than about a hundred people packed together, that could trigger my panic disorder."

Even if someone is genuinely willing to support your recovery, they may need some time to learn and change; they may occasionally forget and need to be corrected. Politely but firmly remind them as you need to—but also cut them some slack and give them time to learn.

To transform these relationships, it might first be important that you do Steps 8 and 9 of the Twelve Steps. List all the things you did that harmed this person (Step 8) and then make amends to the person (Step 9). Remember that making amends means more than apologizing; it means changing your behavior. These two Steps can be the beginning of transforming relationships. (It's a good idea first to talk with your sponsor, your therapist, or a close friend before making direct amends.)

Some people, of course, will tell you flat out that they're not willing to change. Others will agree to change, but won't—even after you've encouraged and reminded them for weeks or months. In either case, for your own health and sanity, you'll need to either limit the relationship or end it. (However, before ending or limiting any relationship—especially early in your recovery—discuss the situation with your therapist or another mental health professional.)

When you decide that it's best for you to end a relationship, remind yourself that it won't be easy; that the other person may respond with anger, insults, accusations, or blame; that how they choose to respond is their responsibility, not yours; and that you are ending the relationship to support your health and recovery. Then take a deep breath and say what you need to say. In some cases, it might be best to let the relationship die on the vine, that is, not say anything but simply stop seeing the person. You may be surprised years later to have the person back in your life.

Afterward, let yourself grieve your loss, and remind yourself that your health and recovery are more important than maintaining an unhealthy relationship.

In practice, it isn't always possible to end an unhealthy relationship—especially one with a relative, co-worker, boss, or employee—without creating some potentially damaging consequences. Sometimes your best option is to maintain a relationship but seriously limit it. Typically, this involves setting and sticking to clear, firm boundaries. ("Marlisa, I can hear how much you're hurting—but no, it's not okay for you to come over right now." "If no alcohol will be served, count me in, but if there will be alcohol, I need to bow out.") Be sure to include your sponsor in your decisions. Your sponsor may have experiences from which you can benefit.

With certain people, you may also need to avoid one-to-one contact as much as possible. ("Please don't call or visit anymore—but I'm happy to talk when we see each other at church." "Toby, would you take Karl to lunch next Thursday? I know how much he spends on us, but he always has too much to drink and starts spouting off about racist stuff. By the time lunch is over, I usually want to get drunk, too.")

Adding to Your Support Network

Your personal support network isn't limited to the people who are already in it. You can ask others to become part of it as your recovery proceeds.

Some of these might be people in your Twelve Step group, or some other support group, whom you've gotten to know—or whom you'd like to know better. Others might be new people you've met since your recovery began. Still others might be relatives you've grown closer to as a result of your recovery and the changes you've made in your life.

Of course, it's always best to ask someone for their support in advance. It's awkward and painful to call someone in an emergency and say, "I know we've never discussed this before, but I need your help, and I need it now!"

Lastly, support is not a one-way street. *Everyone* needs support, not just people with disorders. So don't stop with just asking others for their support; where and when you can, offer yours as well. Whether it's a sympathetic ear, a ride to the airport, or cat-sitting while someone is out of town, there are lots of things—some practical, some emotional—that you can probably do to help.

The Dangers and Temptations of Isolation

By now you know that reaching out and connecting with others—and asking clearly and directly for help when you need it—are essential parts of recovery.

However, one common symptom of many co-occurring disorders is a desire to hide, to retreat from human contact, and to isolate ourselves. This desire is often accompanied by some combination of shame, fear, anxiety, and/or panic. Thoughts like these may bubble up: *Hide yourself away. When you're alone, you don't have to answer anyone, please anyone, or be responsible to anyone. You can't harm or upset anyone, or do the wrong thing, or shame or embarrass yourself. Isolation will bring you safety, familiarity, and comfort.*

This is obviously negative thinking. The truth is that the more we isolate ourselves, the more we feed our illness. We create a downward, inward spiral in which isolation becomes a prison, not a haven, alienating us from people who care about us.

In contrast, connecting with others promotes recovery. Only by taking the risk of reaching out to other human beings can we build and nurture a strong support network, and best support our own healing.

If you see that you are beginning to isolate yourself, the best thing you can do is quickly reach out to someone in your support network. Call them, set up a time to meet, and explain the isolating temptations you're feeling. Better still, do the same with two or three different people.

And don't stop here. In addition, make yourself go to at least one Twelve Step (or other support group) meeting a day, no matter how much you yearn to stay home. At these meetings you will find loving, caring human beings who will understand what you're going through, accept you for who you are, and help you make your way back into the world. Remember this: Your disease is about isolation. Your recovery is about connection.

This chapter hasn't fully discussed the single-most important member of your support network: *you.* You are the person who can provide the most support for your recovery.

In chapter 13, we'll examine what you can do to provide yourself with the best and strongest ongoing support, by creating and following an ideal self-management plan.

Chapter 13

Designing the Right Self-Management Plan

Importance of a Self-Management Plan

Recovery is never an accident. It's the result of many thousands of individual actions taken day by day and breath by breath.

We all know that life rarely goes exactly the way we planned and hoped. But this doesn't mean we should live our lives haphazardly. We all need a basic but flexible structure for daily living. So, just as you created relapse prevention and response plans, it's important that you create a self-management plan that will promote your health, sanity, and recovery. This plan doesn't have to be detailed or complicated. In fact, simpler is usually better.

Developing a self-management plan is you taking an active role in your recovery. You have your treatment professionals to help you with your therapy, medication, and so on. You have your peer recovery support group—like AA—to help with your recovery. But your self-management plan is all about you. You are the key agent—the one who wants the sort of life that is second to none.

Each person's self-management plan is unique, but you might think of it as two inter-related pieces: (1) a list of self-care strategies that you'll follow every day, and (2) a daily schedule that changes from day to day.

Both parts of your self-management plan should be written down. Post your list of self-care strategies in a highly visible spot at home, so you can regularly review it and make sure you're following it. Carry your daily schedule with you in your pocket or purse or attaché case, so you can check it as often as you need to.

Since recovery is not a solo effort, creating a self-management plan isn't a one-person task. Create an initial version on your own, and then run it by some members of your personal support system—close friends and family, your sponsor, your therapist or other treatment professional, and so on. Encourage them to offer comments and suggestions; take what they say seriously; then, with their suggestions in mind, create a final plan.

Most people's self-management plans change over time as their recoveries proceed, and as they change and grow. Give your own self-management plan this flexibility. If at any point something in it no longer supports you or your recovery, change the plan—but do so in consultation with members of your support system.

In addition, throughout your recovery, review—and, if appropriate, update—your self-management plan every three to six months.

Lastly, keep in mind that a plan is a set of commitments, not commandments. If you stop following your plan for a day or two, don't beat yourself up over it. Straying from your plan doesn't make you a failure or a bad person. It's normal for people to occasionally lose their way. You haven't ruined your plan—or your recovery. Pick yourself up, dust yourself off, and begin following your self-management plan once again.

The Foundations of Self-Care

Include most or all of the following in your list of general self-care strategies:

- Get the right amount of sleep.
- Take your medications as prescribed.
- Stay abstinent from drugs and alcohol.
- Regularly spend time with caring people who will support your recovery—and avoid those who won't.
- Pray, meditate, and exercise regularly.
- Eat a healthy diet—but also allow yourself an occasional indulgence.
- Attend Twelve Step and other support group meetings regularly—at least once a week, but three a week is recommended.
- Twice a day, practice mindful relaxation, as you learned to do in chapter 8.
- Have some fun or relaxation each day.

- Regularly take "psychological vitamins"—the positive experiences and activities identified in chapter 9.
- Recognize negative thinking when it appears. Use flexible thinking or STORC to challenge it and replace it with more helpful and accurate thoughts, as you learned.
- Don't forget to get regular checkups from your physician, dentist, eye doctor, and so on.
- If you have a therapist, see this person as planned (not just when you feel like it).
- If you have a psychiatrist, see this person as planned to determine if any of your medications need to be adjusted.
- Avoid people, places, situations, and events that could get in the way of your recovery. Do all you reasonably can to support your recovery.
- Accept yourself while also working to change those things about yourself that you'd like to change.
- Ask for help whenever it's needed. Help others. Paradoxically, one of the best forms of self-care is connecting with and serving other people.

Let's look more closely at a few of these items.

Healthy Eating

What we eat—and don't eat—can raise or lower our energy levels, our resistance to illness, our ability to heal and recover, and our overall physical and mental health. Some foods will support your recovery, while others will inhibit it.

You may already know about healthy eating and proper diet. If so, we recommend that it be a key component of your self-management plan. If not, consult a dietician or nutrition expert to help you build a plan right for you. Remember that cooking can be a great way not only to eat healthy but also to ease stress.

Exercise

Study after study has shown that regular exercise is good for your physical and mental health. This is true no matter what age, size, or shape you are.

In an ideal world, we'd all be able to run, bike, swim, or work out sixty to ninety minutes a day. But more modest exercise—a twenty-minute brisk walk each day—is also quite beneficial. So long as you exercise at least twenty minutes a day, three to five days a week, you'll see a noticeable benefit.

Sleep

Getting the right amount of sleep is an essential element of good self-care. Yet most people don't get all the sleep they need.

The typical adult needs eight full hours of sleep each day. Some people, particularly those who do a lot of physical or creative work, need as much as nine or ten. The medications you take for your mental health may make you drowsier than normal. Here are some tips to help you get the sleep you need:

- As you create your daily schedule, allow for at least eight hours of sleep daily—more, if you feel you need it. (But if even nine hours isn't enough, check with your psychiatrist, therapist, or other treatment professional. Your medications may be making you tired, in which case they should probably be adjusted.)
- If possible, include an afternoon nap in your daily schedule. For most people, it's actually healthier to take a twenty- to sixty-minute nap in the afternoon and sleep less during the night than it is to sleep eight straight hours once a day. In fact, many people find that for every minute they nap during the day, they need two or three fewer minutes of sleep at night. (If you start to have trouble falling asleep at night, however, stop taking naps.)
- As much as possible, go to bed and get up at the same times every day.
- Exercise regularly. Many studies show that exercise helps people sleep better.
- Do something relaxing during the thirty to forty-five minutes before you go to sleep. Read, listen to music, take a bath, meditate, pray, watch the sky, and so on.
- Avoid drinking caffeinated beverages after 6:00 p.m. (or after 4:00 p.m. if you're sensitive to caffeine). Keep in mind that black tea, colas, many other soft drinks, some sport drinks, and most energy drinks all contain caffeine.
- Avoid tobacco for at least three hours before going to sleep.
- If you find yourself lying awake and unable to fall asleep for more than thirty minutes, try mindful relaxation, as you learned to do in chapter 8.

Spiritual Practices

Attend and *participate* in Twelve Step meetings on a regular basis. Three meetings a week is recommended for those in early recovery. Even more meetings may be necessary during times of high stress. Research shows that those who not only attend but also participate in Twelve Step meetings will be more successful in their recovery. To participate means to have a sponsor, arrive early at meetings to help set up chairs or start the coffee, welcome newcomers to your meeting, offer to lead a meeting, and do other things as an active member. Meditation, prayer, and other mindfulness practices can also help you reduce stress and relax. They also support (and sometimes improve) your overall physical and mental health. And they can open the heart and encourage spiritual insight. A spiritual ritual may involve simply reading a meditation book for fifteen minutes every morning.

Fun and Leisure

Many Americans don't include enough fun and leisure in their lives. This is a shame because, in moderate amounts, fun, leisure, and relaxation are all very healthy.

In particular, we Americans have lost our appreciation for a sabbath—that one day each week when we disengage from the working world, relax, have fun, and attend to matters of the spirit. Instead, in the twenty-first century, we fill our weekends with work, shopping, errands, our kids' sporting events, and other obligations.

Try to buck this trend and make one day a week into your own unique sabbath. This doesn't have to be Sunday (or Saturday). It doesn't even have to be the same day every week.

An alternative is to reserve an hour in your schedule each and every day specifically for relaxation and fun. Better still, do both, so you have a sabbath every week and a mini-sabbath once a day.

Of course, make sure that what you do for fun and relaxation supports your recovery. And be careful to avoid people, places, situations, and events that could trigger craving and encourage relapse.

Your Daily Schedule

Keeping a daily schedule helps you create a healthy balance of work, fun, relationships, and recovery-oriented activities. It also makes life easier to handle. In fact, some people with co-occurring disorders say that their daily schedule is one of their best recovery tools.

A daily schedule also provides these benefits:

- It helps you stay on track and do the things you know are good for you.
- It helps you prioritize your time and activities.
- It helps you manage your time throughout the day.
- It enables you to remember appointments, meetings, and other activities. This is especially helpful if you are taking medications that affect your memory.
- It helps you become more realistic about how long things take and how much time you have available.
- It tells you at a glance whether you are following your own self-care principles.
- It reduces both boredom and depression. It's harder to be bored or depressed when you're busy.

It doesn't matter whether you use a daily planner, a datebook, a spiral notebook, the scheduling software on your computer, or something else entirely. Whatever you use, you'll be pleased and surprised at how much easier it makes your life—and how much it supports your recovery.

Here are some other tips for creating and using a daily schedule:

- You don't need to account for every minute. Think in fifteen-minute and thirty-minute blocks.
- Your schedule is a simple tool—so, as AA says, "Keep it simple."
- You don't need to follow the exact same schedule every day. Your schedule can be as regular or as varied from day to day as you need it to be.
- Be realistic about how long things actually take. Keep in mind that most things will take longer than you expect—sometimes much longer. In addition, often there will be unexpected waits and delays, such as rush-hour traffic or construction delays.
- Don't overbook yourself. Deliberately leave some empty slots in your schedule. This creates helpful buffers between tasks and events.
- If you tend to worry, try setting aside half an hour a day as your "worry time." During that half hour, fret about anything and everything you like. But when

the time is up, your worrying time is over—now stop worrying and get back to your life in the here and now. If you catch yourself worrying at other times, tell yourself, *Okay, during my next worry session, I'll worry about this. But right now there are other things I need to focus on.*

Self-Care versus Self-Indulgence

Understanding the differences between care and comfort is enormously important. Most of us can confuse comfort with self-care. Some activities—healthy eating, regular exercise, taking your medications on schedule, and so on—are unquestionably forms of self-care. Others—frequently staying in bed all day, eating an entire box of cookies in one sitting, and so on—are just as undeniably self-indulgences or comforts that could hinder your recovery.

But in between self-care and self-indulgence can be a large gray area. If you take yourself out for dinner to celebrate two years of sobriety, is that a form of self-care? It certainly could be. But it isn't if you eat it at 1:00 a.m. and you need to be at work at 7:00. Sometimes an activity that is self-care in one situation can be self-indulgence in another. Or something is self-care when it's done in moderation, but can become self-indulgent when done too often or too long.

For example, getting a professional massage once a week/month is a wonderful form of self-care—but not if it's going to bust your budget and make you unable to pay your rent. Running two miles a day may boost your energy, but running four might make you too tired to do your job well.

If you're uncertain whether *any* activity, event, or decision qualifies as self-care, simply ask yourself, *Does this support my sanity, health, and recovery?* If the answer is yes, go for it. If the answer is no, stop where you are and take a different, healthier path. If you don't know, ask two or three people in your personal support network for reality checks.

In the gray area between self-care and self-indulgence are the near-equivalent *self-soothing* and *self-comfort.* Mental health professionals often recommend these, especially for people who are feeling down or upset. But you need to be careful and discerning. Ask yourself, *Will this self-soothing activity help or hinder my recovery?* If it will help, or clearly won't hurt, feel free to do it. But if it will hurt, stop right there! Use your flexible thinking skills to determine how your thinking has gone astray and what alternative activity you might do instead.

One common symptom of many mental health and substance use disorders is this form of negative thinking: *If it feels good, it must be good for me and my recovery. I'll do it!* (Sounds a lot like Homer Simpson, doesn't it?) At times you will need to use your flexible thinking skills to catch and correct such stinking thinking before it affects what you do.

As your recovery proceeds, it will be time for you to engage fully with the world once again. You may decide to look for a job, find new friends, begin dating, or otherwise resume participation in the full spectrum of human affairs. Chapter 14 will provide practical strategies and tips for reentering the stream of life without endangering your recovery.

CHAPTER 14

Finding a Place in the World

Fitting In

Finding a place in the world is not only an important element of recovery; it's part of everyone's personal journey. Each of us must find our own answer to the question "How and where do I fit into the world?"—and any satisfying answer must be simultaneously practical, psychological, spiritual, and existential.

Many people with mental health and substance use disorders struggle with this question. In fact, some people drank and used drugs in hopes of feeling "at home" and more comfortable in the world. Of course, the more they drank and used, the less "at home" they felt and the more separated and lost they became. Some used to have a comfortable place in the world—but because of their disorders, everything fell apart, and now they need to rethink and remake their lives.

Other people with co-occurring disorders feel they've *never* had a place in the world. This very lack of security may even have contributed to their disorders. Yet now, in recovery, they sense that such a place may exist after all—or that they can create it.

Finding a place in the world involves trial and error, intuition and discernment, success and failure, love and effort. It requires us to draw on the skills we have learned and the knowledge we have gleaned—yet it also requires us to feel our way forward, step by step, one day at a time, into an unknown future that our recovery helps shape.

In this regard, people recovering from co-occurring disorders have an advantage over many other people. They've experienced for themselves just how uncertain and change-able life can be. As a result, they may feel less shock and surprise when life throws them a curveball. Interestingly, it has been said that people in recovery have been to hell and back, and everyone else is trying to avoid going there. Indeed, most people in recovery are not victims—they are survivors.

Yet most people—not just those with co-occurring disorders—sometimes have to re-think and remake their lives. Some do it multiple times: they get divorced, change careers, leave their homelands for new and unknown places, and redefine their work and missions in life. So, if you have to start over, reinvent yourself, or remake your life, know that you are in good company. Millions of people face the same challenges and stand in solidarity with you.

General Tips for Reengaging with the World

Here are tips for people with co-occurring disorders who are attempting to find their way in the world. They are intended as friendly reminders, clues, and hints:

- Much of what happens to us is outside of our control. So, instead of trying to control other people or the world, focus on those things you *can* control: your own actions and decisions. Remember the Serenity Prayer: "the courage to change the things I can." Practice acceptance.
- It's essential to set goals. The best goals are ones that you can achieve, but only with some effort and stretching.
- If what looked like a good goal turns out to be impossible, or too easy, or no longer helpful, replace it with a better one.
- Be flexible. It's important—and helpful—to make plans. But be willing to amend those plans if your situation changes—or if your original plans prove less than helpful.
- When you see trouble or danger is heading your way, don't freeze up. Get out of harm's way quickly, and if you need help, ask for it immediately. Have your sponsor's phone number handy. Or call a friend.
- Don't try to force solutions. Do your best; then let go of the outcome. "You're responsible for the effort not the outcome" and "Progress, not perfection," say many in Twelve Step groups.
- Take reasonable risks. Don't take unreasonable ones.

- Use your mindful relaxation, flexible thinking, and STORC CBT skills whenever they can be helpful.
- Ask for help when you need it. This includes using your personal support network, but it also means asking people outside of that network for help as well. One common trait of successful people is that they regularly ask others for what they want or need. Practice asking for help on little things, so when the big things come, you'll find it easier to ask for help.
- Be patient. Rebuilding a life takes time. In fact, most good things take more time and effort than we want, hope, or expect them to.
- No one knows exactly how his or her life will unfold. No one has enough information to be a pessimist. Your life will be full of surprises, just like everyone else's. Each new surprise is an opportunity to learn and grow. Sometimes the best things happen for us when it seems like we didn't get what we wanted. (Some of the worst things may have happened for us when we *did* get what we wanted.)
- Life can only be lived in the present. Stay in the here and now, and deal with what's in front of you. Take things one day—and, when necessary, one hour— at a time.

Citizenship

Being a good citizen is a wonderful way to meet new people, contribute to the world, and work your way back into it, all at the same time. You might consider it as part of your Twelve Step service work.

Almost every service organization can use more volunteers. If you contact one of these organizations and offer to volunteer, chances are good that you'll be welcomed, thanked enthusiastically, and quickly put to work. In those rare instances where no more volunteers are needed, you'll be referred to another organization or program that needs your help.

Some excellent places to volunteer include the following:

- nearby hospital or nursing home
- local food pantry
- local animal shelter
- nearby homeless shelter

- church, synagogue, mosque, or other religious or spiritual center
- your neighborhood association and/or city government
- regional office of National Alliance on Mental Illness (NAMI)
- your Twelve Step group (or other support group)
- regional offices for AA, NA, or other Twelve Step programs
- art museums, orchestras, and other arts organizations
- any other nonprofit organization, large or small—if there's a cause you believe in, there's probably a nonprofit organization that works to further it and could use your help
- campaign office of a political candidate you support
- your political party
- your own extended family—maybe an aunt or uncle needs the roof fixed, the garden weeded, or some friendly company on Sunday nights

Most often, you don't need any special skills to volunteer. In fact, in many organizations, the biggest need is for volunteers who will do simple, everyday tasks. If you can read to people, pack or unpack boxes, mow lawns, pick up trash, wash windows, plant or water flowers, stuff envelopes, run errands, or cook, serve, or deliver meals, there are many organizations that could use your help. There are, however, many places that could also utilize some of your professional work skills.

Being a good citizen has many benefits. The community benefits, and you "get out of yourself," forget your troubles, and connect with other people. All good stuff.

Renewing and Reestablishing Old Relationships

If you're like most people in recovery, some of the people you were once close to have pulled away because of your disorders. Or, perhaps, you pushed *them* away with your drinking, drugging, and erratic behavior.

Once you're well into your recovery, it may be time to reach out to some of these people once again—and, in some cases, to try to mend your relationships with them. If you're working the Twelve Steps, working Steps 6 through 9 can be extremely helpful in amending your past relationships. You might consider first making a list of people you have harmed in your life. Before making direct amends and contacting these people, it's best if you speak to someone, such as your sponsor, counselor, spiritual adviser, or close friend. Afterward, when you're ready, consider contacting the people on the list, apologizing for your past behavior, explaining that you're in recovery, and offering to make amends. People familiar with making amends—and who isn't?—can help you. Sponsors can offer you many tips and suggestions.

Creating New Relationships

Once your mental health and substance use disorders become manageable, you're in an ideal situation to begin building some new relationships.

Your Twelve Step group (or other support group) is one excellent place to start. Because these folks are in recovery themselves, they can empathize with you and act in ways that support your recovery.

Also consider attending larger Twelve Step social events. These might include multi-group events such as picnics and potlucks, as well as regional events, such as conferences, conventions, and roundups. At these events you can meet new people, begin new friendships, and support your recovery, all at the same time.

As you build these new relationships, be discerning but not picky. It's essential that any new relationship be with someone who will support your recovery. But don't require people to be perfect, or to exactly fit your ideal of what a friend should be. In real life, strong friendships are often forged between people who have very different personalities.

For many people in recovery, building new relationships includes dating. An important piece of advice about dating is this: take it slow. As tempting and as exciting as it can be to rush into a new relationship—or to become intimate with someone attractive—the reality is that moving too fast often creates problems. Taking it slow has exactly the opposite effect: it helps people build trust and intimacy—maintain their serenity and recoveries—even as the fires of romance burn steadily higher. These relationships are very important and can bring out the best and worst in us. Most of us have much to learn about how these relationships work. So take your time.

In addition to mending old relationships and forging new ones, consider ways to improve your own skills, knowledge, and interests. These, too, can help you reconnect with the community and the world at large. Now is a great time to begin exploring your interests. If you've always wanted to work with clay, sign up for a beginning pottery class. If you want to become more limber and relaxed, take a beginning yoga class. If you've always wanted to learn photography, register for an introductory photography class.

A big bonus of each class will be the new people you'll meet in it. Some of them will likely be interesting—and, because you're in the same class, you'll already have at least one interest in common. From this common interest, new friendships may blossom.

When Do You Tell Someone That You Have Co-occurring Disorders?

As you meet new people, build closer relationships, and make new professional connections, you'll need to decide whom to tell about your mental health and substance use disorders—and how, when, and exactly what to tell them.

You already know that there's no set of simple rules for revealing this information, and that you'll need to decide on a case-by-case basis. Nevertheless, these guidelines can be helpful:

- In general, you don't need to rush to tell others about your disorders. Remember, it's not something to feel guilty or ashamed about—and it's not contagious.
- Some people find it useful to imagine that they have some other form of chronic illness, such as diabetes, hypertension, or asthma. Then they ask themselves, *"When would I tell someone that I have* that *disorder?"* The same answer might apply to your co-occurring disorders.
- Once you've begun to grow close to someone, either as a friend or a romantic partner, it's best to tell them about your disorders. Otherwise, it becomes a secret, and the other person may feel that you haven't been honest and forthright with them. Most people won't want, need, or expect a lot of detail. Do, however, offer to answer any questions they might have. All other considerations aside, if someone suggests an activity that will undermine your recovery ("Want to smoke some dope?" or "Want to stop at the bar for a drink?"), you owe it to your health and sanity to say no—and to explain why.
- When telling people about your disorders, be sure to also explain that you're in recovery. You can also add details such as "I completed treatment last fall, and I've been clean and sober for nine months now" or "My meds have worked very well. I haven't had any serious symptoms since I started taking them last winter."
- Be clear, straightforward, and matter-of-fact. For example: "I'm sure you've noticed that I avoid bars. That's because I'm in recovery from alcoholism and post-traumatic stress disorder. I've successfully completed treatment. I've been

clean and sober for nineteen months now, and I've been managing the PTSD well. But part of staying clean and sober includes staying away from triggering events and situations. For me that includes bars. So I'd like to sit outside on the patio instead."

- Consult with others—such as your sponsor, therapist, and/or close friend—about disclosing personal information when interviewing for a job or during other critical situations.

As your recovery proceeds, many things in your life will likely change for the better: your physical and mental health, your relationships, your feelings about yourself and others, and your hope for the future. Still, your life will most likely continue to have the usual ups and downs, and both wonderful and terrible surprises, simply because you're human.

Recovery leads to a better, fuller life—but it doesn't lead to paradise. Good and bad things will happen. These ebbs and flows are woven into the very fabric of life.

Patience and a long-term perspective are both essential elements of progress in recovery. In the middle of life's inevitable ups and downs, we can recognize—and regularly remind ourselves—that our own lives are slowly and steadily improving. No longer is the world we live in an illusion distorted by alcohol, drugs, and wild emotional states. But instead, one day at a time we are reclaiming our equilibrium, sanity, sobriety, and serenity. One day at a time, we are building a spiritual home for ourselves in this world.

Recommended Resources

Helpful Books

Alcoholics Anonymous (fourth edition)
Alcoholics Anonymous World Services, Inc., 2001
This is the most recent edition of the famous "Big Book"—the classic volume that gave rise to the Twelve Step movement.

At Wit's End: What You Need to Know When a Loved One Is Diagnosed with Addiction and Mental Illness
Jeff Jay and Jerry A. Boriskin, Ph.D.
Hazelden, 2007
An ideal book to give to family and friends.

Clinical Psychopharmacology Made Ridiculously Simple (sixth edition)
John Preston, Psy.D., and James Johnson, M.D.
MedMaster, 2009
A user-friendly guide to the drugs used to treat mental health disorders and substance use disorders.

Easy Does It Dating Guide: For People in Recovery
Mary Faulkner
Hazelden, 2004
The only dating guide written specifically for people in recovery. Faulkner has also
written *Easy Does It Relationship Guide* (Hazelden, 2007).

Making Them Pay: How to Get the Most from Health Insurance and Managed Care
Rhonda Orin
St. Martin's Press, 2001
An empowering and money-saving tool for anyone with health insurance
or HMO coverage.

The Road Less Traveled: A New Psychology of Love, Traditional Values, and Spiritual Growth
M. Scott Peck, M.D.
Simon & Schuster, 1978
This highly successful book incorporates love, science, and religion into a discussion of
personal growth.

Today I Will Do One Thing: Daily Readings for Awareness and Hope
Tim Mc.
Hazelden, 1995
Contains 366 meditations written for people with co-occurring disorders.

*The Twelve Steps and Dual Disorders: A Framework of Recovery for Those of Us with
Addiction and an Emotional or Psychiatric Illness*
Tim Hamilton and Pat Samples
Hazelden, 1994
A guide to applying each of the Twelve Steps to co-occurring disorders.

Twelve Steps and Twelve Traditions
Alcoholics Anonymous World Services, Inc., 1981
Originally published in 1952, this classic book lays out the principles by which
Twelve Step members recover and Twelve Step fellowships operate.

A User's Guide to Therapy: What to Expect and How You Can Benefit
Tamara L. Kaiser
Norton, 2008
An excellent, highly readable guide to finding, working with, and getting the most from a therapist.

Useful Web Sites

General Information on Mental Health, Substance Use,
and Co-occurring Disorders

American Psychiatric Association
www.psych.org
(Most of APA's information for consumers is at www.healthyminds.org.)

American Psychological Association
www.apa.org

Cleveland Clinic
www.clevelandclinic.org

Dual Diagnosis Website (privately owned site run by Kathleen Sciacca)
users.erols.com/ksciacca
(A directory of programs and people that treat co-occurring disorders is at cgibin.erols.com/ksciacca/cgi-bin/db.cgi.)

Mayo Clinic
www.mayoclinic.com

Mental Health America (formerly National Mental Health Association)
www.nmha.org

National Alliance on Mental Illness (NAMI)
www.nami.org

National Clearinghouse for Alcohol and Drug Information
ncadi.samhsa.gov

National Institute on Drug Abuse (NIDA)
www.nida.nih.gov

National Institutes of Health
www.health.nih.gov

Substance Abuse and Mental Health Services Administration (SAMHSA)
www.samhsa.gov

Web MD
www.webmd.com

National Offices of Twelve Step Programs

Alcoholics Anonymous
www.aa.org

Cocaine Anonymous
www.ca.org

Crystal Meth Anonymous
www.crystalmeth.org

Double Trouble in Recovery
www.doubletroubleinrecovery.org

Dual Diagnosis Anonymous
www.ddaoforegon.org

Dual Recovery Anonymous
www.draonline.org

Emotions Anonymous
www.emotionsanonymous.org

Heroin Anonymous
www.heroin-anonymous.org

Marijuana Anonymous
www.marijuana-anonymous.org

Narcotics Anonymous
www.na.org

About the Author

Mark McGovern, Ph.D., is an associate professor of Psychiatry and of Community and Family Medicine at Dartmouth Medical School. He joined Dartmouth in 2001 after fifteen years on the faculty of the Department of Psychiatry and Behavioral Sciences at Northwestern University Medical School in Chicago, Illinois. He began his professional career as a counselor in an inner city detoxification program in North Philadelphia in 1978. Dr. McGovern specializes in the treatment of co-occurring substance use and psychiatric disorders and practices through the Department of Psychiatry at the Dartmouth-Hitchcock Medical Center. He has studied and published widely in the area of addiction treatment services research. He has conducted treatment research in a variety of settings, including addiction treatment programs, community mental health centers, state psychiatric hospitals, academic medical centers, office-based practices, private specialty treatment programs, and state addiction and mental health treatment delivery systems. Dr. McGovern has worked extensively with special populations, including impaired health care professionals and the National Football League's Program for Substance Abuse. He has also conducted training and research in the assessment and treatment of the dual-diagnosis patient in both psychiatric and addiction treatment systems. In July of 2004, he received a career development award from the National Institute on Drug Abuse. The overarching goal of this award involves developing, testing, and transferring evidence-based treatments to community settings for persons with co-occurring substance use and psychiatric disorders.

Hazelden, a national nonprofit organization founded in 1949, helps people reclaim their lives from the disease of addiction. Built on decades of knowledge and experience, Hazelden offers a comprehensive approach to addiction that addresses the full range of patient, family, and professional needs, including treatment and continuing care for youth and adults, research, higher learning, public education and advocacy, and publishing.

A life of recovery is lived "one day at a time." Hazelden publications, both educational and inspirational, support and strengthen lifelong recovery. In 1954, Hazelden published *Twenty-Four Hours a Day,* the first daily meditation book for recovering alcoholics, and Hazelden continues to publish works to inspire and guide individuals in treatment and recovery, and their loved ones. Professionals who work to prevent and treat addiction also turn to Hazelden for evidence-based curricula, informational materials, and videos for use in schools, treatment programs, and correctional programs.

Through published works, Hazelden extends the reach of hope, encouragement, help, and support to individuals, families, and communities affected by addiction and related issues.

For questions about Hazelden publications, please call **800-328-9000** or visit us online at **hazelden.org/bookstore**.